What is a Mind Map?

Wikipedia tells us that "A **mind map** is a diagram used to visually organize information." Well, yes, it is that, but it is so much more. Mind Maps have been used in the business world for some time. They are used by individuals as well as groups. And they are "diagrams used to visually organize information."

A mind maps starts with a seed, and, like a tree, grows a trunk and then branches and leaves. Each new area of growth is w new idea that is discovered. I have used mind maps for taking notes both in seminary and in law school. My mind thinks visually. I memorize concepts visually. I am right-brained in that way. But mind maps are not just for us right-brainiacs.

There is a logic to them that will stimulate the left-brainiacs as well. I have written my life story as a mind map. Some people use a mind map to build their family tree. Some authors use mind maps to plan their next novel. I am a preacher, I used mind maps to prepare sermons and preach them. Preaching with a manuscript does not work for me. I find that I spend more time on the wording than I do the meaning. And I feel like a slave to the manuscript.

You will find there are more drawings in this book than words, although my drawing has words. But if I want to tell the funny story about the seagull to bring across my point, I may just write "seagull", or, even better, put a picture of a seagull on the map.

Although mind maps have been around for years, it was Tony Buzan who popularized them on his BBC TV series "Use Your Head." Since then many have jumped on the bandwagon. Some mind maps are done freehand. Others use a specific computer mind map program, of which there are too many to count. I often like to draw them freehand, although for the purposes of this book (and my website www.sermonmindmaps.com), I use a program called "Lucidchart." Of all of the computer programs, I find it the easiest and most complete, for my purposes. I can add pictures, shapes, lines, colors and etc. I would not, however, discount the fact that you may find a program that works better for you.

How to Prepare Sermons through Mind Mapping

I design my sermon through mind mapping and take the mind map with me to the pulpit. Sometimes I look at it if I have a long quote. But you will find that it is much easier to memorize your sermon easier using a mind map. Perhaps "memorize" is not a good word, "visualize" is what you are actually doing. This book and the diagrams are in black and white, but before I preach the sermon, I take out my colored markers and go to town. Different colors are given to different points. This will also help with memory. Sometimes I feel like a little kid with my crayons. No one said preparing a sermon can't be fun.

This does not mean that the sermon needs to be "topical". I have used mind maps to flesh out texts. I give you an example of this later in the book in a sermon called "The Christian's To Do List". Whether expository or topical, you can use mind maps to squeeze out the juice of the text or topic. Oftentimes the text itself will set the pattern for the mind map.

Let's take a topic and try mind mapping it. There is no better topic than love. And to make it easier let's ask the questions: What? Who? When? Why? And How? You could use, as your main text, John 13 or 1 Corinthians 13 or 1 John 4 to name only a few passages on the topic of love. Let's look at the diagram and then I will explain it.

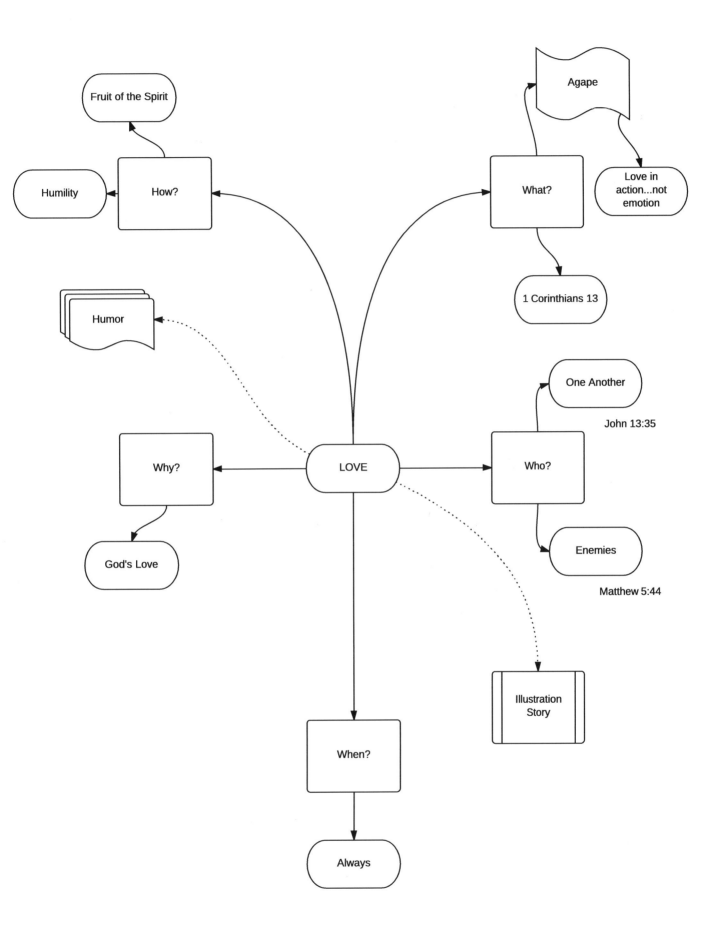

Notice that I have the main topic in the middle, with What, Who, When, Why and How as my first branches of the mind map. The first question is "What"? I have "Agape" and a branch flowing from it that explains it. You could add "eros", "philia" and "storge" if you want to show the other Greek words and their different meanings. This branch is part of a sermon, but can easily be a sermon in itself.

Then comes the question "Who"? Then you see the branches "One Another" which can be based on John 13:15 or John 15; and "Enemies" which we find in Matthew 5.

This may be a good time to give an illustration to highlight the "What" and "Who" of love. Tell a story that fleshes out the 2 questions (or just one of them).

I believe the rest of the mind map is self-explanatory. "When" can be backed up in many verses. 1 John can back up the "Why?" question. And "How?" can lead into "The Fruit of the Spirit" or 1 Corinthians 13. You can add more branches to each. I have also added a place for humor. This sermon is deep and can get exhausting. Sometime throwing in a little humor can help to give the congregation a breather, while still illustrating your point(s).

As I mentioned before, this can be one sermon, or a whole series of sermons on "Love".

One illustration can be about the mother who told her son that she would give him a quarter if he polished her shoes. He said he would and she gave him the quarter. He spent all morning polishing the shoes with great care and determination. A few hours later when his mother put her newly polished shoes on she noticed that was something stuck in one of them. She reached in and pulled out a quarter and a note that read: "You can keep the quarter, I done it for love." Then you can say that love does not look for rewards. This is agape love…love in action.

This gives you a simple approach to preparing a sermon using the mind map technique.

Now let's talk for a moment about preaching from a mind map. You can carry the mind map with you to the pulpit, or, since it is laid out so logically, the points are easily memorized. It is much easier to memorize a mind map than a manuscript.

There are times when I write a manuscript after I have made my mind map. Then I take the manuscript and write out a more complete mind map. Find the way that is right for you.

A note on pictures: You can easily find an image of a shoe (or a quarter) and simply paste it to your mind map to remind you of the illustration of the shoe I wrote above.

In the following pages, I have included 30 sermon mind maps that you can use. You will note that on some there are #'s to guide you concerning the progression of points. Usually I begin with the Introduction at the top of the map, and then I move in a clockwise pattern. The conclusion is usually on the top left.

ABC'S OF LOVING YOURSELF

Some people think they can never change. Some people think they don't need to change. Which one are you?
God has a transformation ready for you. God has a new calling for you. God has a new boldness for you to step into, a new role God is calling you into.

Accepting Christ involves knowing God accepts you. Through believing that you are saved by His work on the cross rather than your work on earth, you "accept Christ." By relying upon the Gospel of forgiveness rather than the Law's demands, you "accept Christ" as your Savior. But it all begins with knowing what God did to accept you.
If you don't feel worthy to be in God's family, don't worry. That is actually a healthy and accurate perspective. The truth is that none of us are worthy. But God's acceptance of us is not based on our "worthiness," but on Christ's sacrifice. It is only because of Jesus and His death on the cross that God accepts you. *Christ died for sins once for all, the righteous for the unrighteous, to bring you to God.*" (1 Peter 3:18)

Illustration: Seagulls are marvelous birds.

God has made us accepted in the Beloved.
Ephesians 1:6 (NKJV)

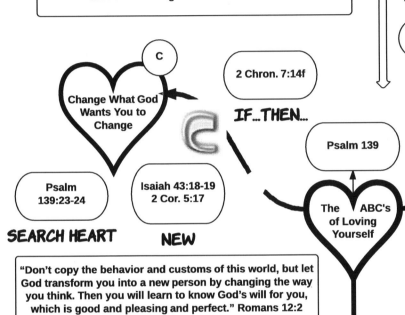

C — **Change What God Wants You to Change**

2 Chron. 7:14f

IF...THEN...

Psalm 139

A — **Accept that God Accepts you**

Rom. 15:7

Psalm 139:23-24

Isaiah 43:18-19
2 Cor. 5:17

The ABC's of Loving Yourself

SEARCH HEART

NEW

"Don't copy the behavior and customs of this world, but let God transform you into a new person by changing the way you think. Then you will learn to know God's will for you, which is good and pleasing and perfect." Romans 12:2

Many of us base our self confidence on what other people think, so we work hard at being accepted. We buy things, we wear things, we join things -- all just for the benefit of trying to be accepted by our friends, family, co-workers and peers.
But our verse today says God has already accepted us in Jesus Christ.
Does God say you have to earn the acceptance? That you could ever deserve it? No. The Bible just says, God has accepted you.
If you're a believer, then you've accepted Jesus into your life. But do you understand that God accepts you? He loves you unconditionally and accepts you for who you are.
Psalm 27:10 says, "Even if my mother and father forsake me, the Lord will receive me."

Ted Winn: God Believes in You
(lyrics): I know they hurt you
Said you would never make it
Some did desert you
You feel you can't take it
But He didn't bring you this far to let you fail
Cause God believes in you
Sometimes life pressures they get so heavy
But you can't give up and forfeit your destiny
See he gave you dreams and now you must pursue
God Believes (God Believes)
God Believes (God Believes)
Yes he does
And that's why you made it through, through your storms
God was on your side, protecting you all along
And whatever he promised you, he will
Listen, God believes, I'm saying
God believes, God believes

Disciples/Simon Peter

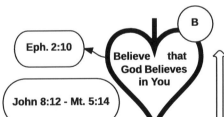

B — **Believe that God Believes in You**

Eph. 2:10

John 8:12 - Mt. 5:14

"I have no other plan."

God sometimes pushes us to our limits because he has greater faith in us than we have in ourselves

Approval/Acceptance: If that's the case -- with your parents or with anyone else in your life you've been seeking to please -- there are two things you need to know:
In all likelihood, you're never going to get that approval or acceptance. Not because of who you are but because of who they are.
You don't need their approval because you are acceptable to God. You don't need their approval to be happy.
What a relief that is to understand. **You only need the love and approval of one person, and you already have it: GOD SAYS YOU ARE ACCEPTABLE!**

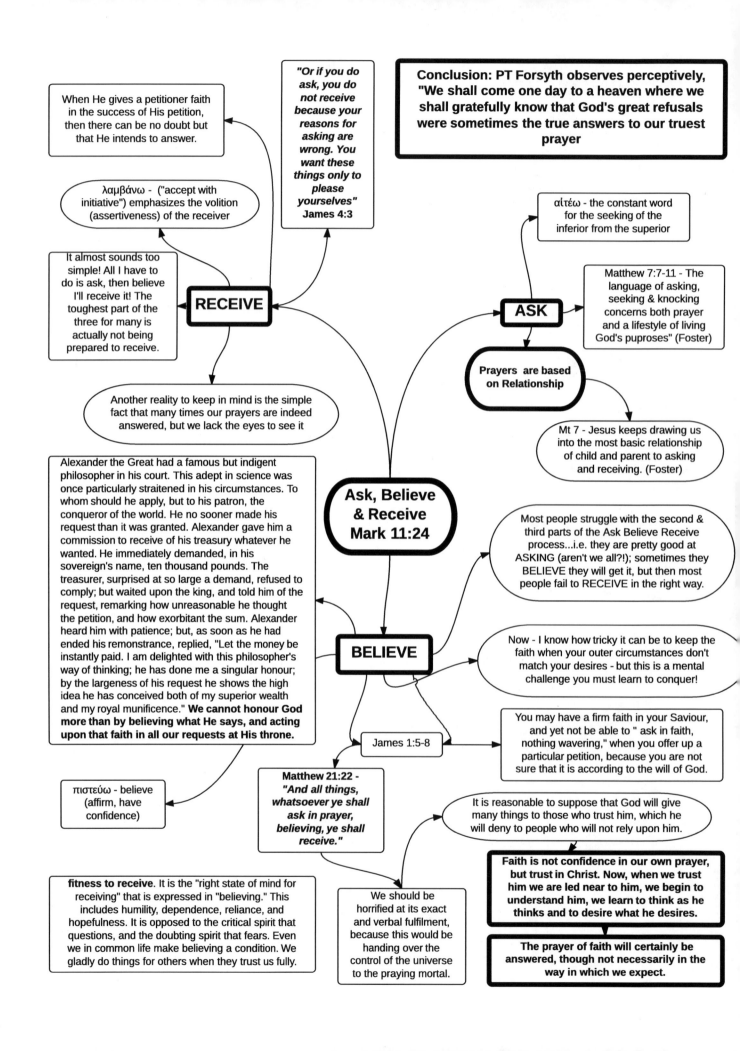

Ask, Believe & Receive Mark 11:24

ASK

αἰτέω - the constant word for the seeking of the inferior from the superior

Matthew 7:7-11 - The language of asking, seeking & knocking concerns both prayer and a lifestyle of living God's puproses" (Foster)

Prayers are based on Relationship

Mt 7 - Jesus keeps drawing us into the most basic relationship of child and parent to asking and receiving. (Foster)

Conclusion: PT Forsyth observes perceptively, "We shall come one day to a heaven where we shall gratefully know that God's great refusals were sometimes the true answers to our truest prayer

RECEIVE

When He gives a petitioner faith in the success of His petition, then there can be no doubt but that He intends to answer.

λαμβάνω - ("accept with initiative") emphasizes the volition (assertiveness) of the receiver

"Or if you do ask, you do not receive because your reasons for asking are wrong. You want these things only to please yourselves" James 4:3

It almost sounds too simple! All I have to do is ask, then believe I'll receive it! The toughest part of the three for many is actually not being prepared to receive.

Another reality to keep in mind is the simple fact that many times our prayers are indeed answered, but we lack the eyes to see it

Most people struggle with the second & third parts of the Ask Believe Receive process...i.e. they are pretty good at ASKING (aren't we all?!); sometimes they BELIEVE they will get it, but then most people fail to RECEIVE in the right way.

Now - I know how tricky it can be to keep the faith when your outer circumstances don't match your desires - but this is a mental challenge you must learn to conquer!

BELIEVE

Alexander the Great had a famous but indigent philosopher in his court. This adept in science was once particularly straitened in his circumstances. To whom should he apply, but to his patron, the conqueror of the world. He no sooner made his request than it was granted. Alexander gave him a commission to receive of his treasury whatever he wanted. He immediately demanded, in his sovereign's name, ten thousand pounds. The treasurer, surprised at so large a demand, refused to comply; but waited upon the king, and told him of the request, remarking how unreasonable he thought the petition, and how exorbitant the sum. Alexander heard him with patience; but, as soon as he had ended his remonstrance, replied, "Let the money be instantly paid. I am delighted with this philosopher's way of thinking; he has done me a singular honour; by the largeness of his request he shows the high idea he has conceived both of my superior wealth and my royal munificence." **We cannot honour God more than by believing what He says, and acting upon that faith in all our requests at His throne.**

πιστεύω - believe (affirm, have confidence)

James 1:5-8

Matthew 21:22 - *"And all things, whatsoever ye shall ask in prayer, believing, ye shall receive."*

You may have a firm faith in your Saviour, and yet not be able to " ask in faith, nothing wavering," when you offer up a particular petition, because you are not sure that it is according to the will of God.

It is reasonable to suppose that God will give many things to those who trust him, which he will deny to people who will not rely upon him.

Faith is not confidence in our own prayer, but trust in Christ. Now, when we trust him we are led near to him, we begin to understand him, we learn to think as he thinks and to desire what he desires.

The prayer of faith will certainly be answered, though not necessarily in the way in which we expect.

fitness to receive. It is the "right state of mind for receiving" that is expressed in "believing." This includes humility, dependence, reliance, and hopefulness. It is opposed to the critical spirit that questions, and the doubting spirit that fears. Even we in common life make believing a condition. We gladly do things for others when they trust us fully.

We should be horrified at its exact and verbal fulfilment, because this would be handing over the control of the universe to the praying mortal.

Life is easier than you think...
All you have to do is
Accept the impossible
Do without the indispensable
Bear the intolerable...and...Be
able to smile at anything

"Happiness is,,," ---depends on outside events

HAPPINESS IS

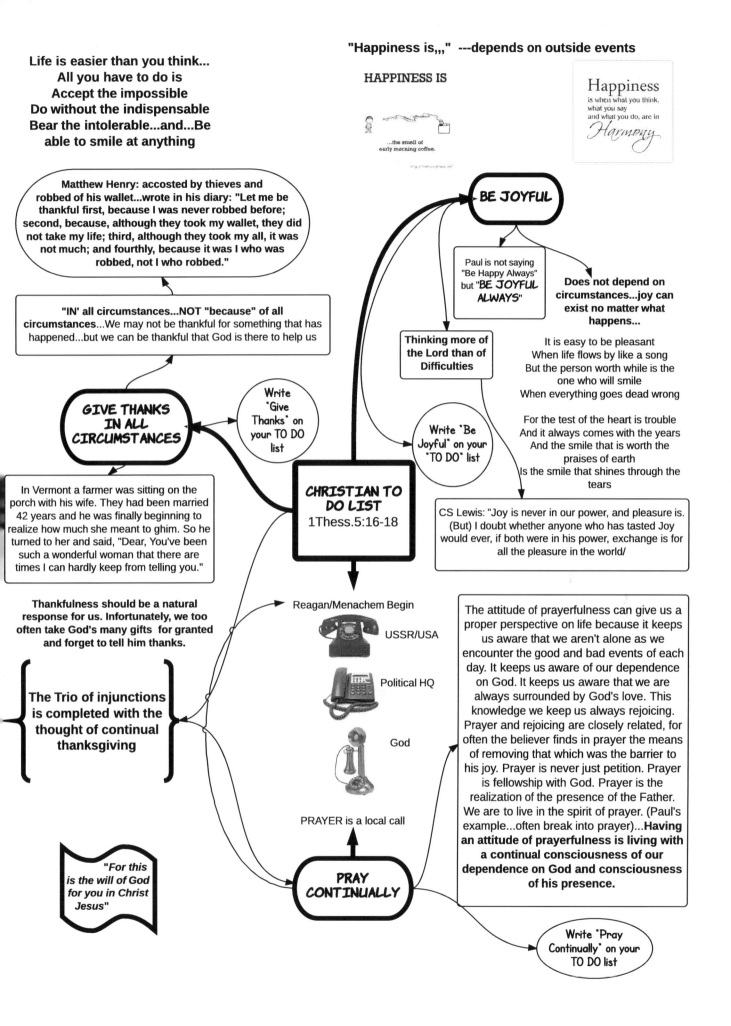

...the smell of
early morning coffee.

Happiness
is when what you think,
what you say
and what you do, are in
Harmony

Matthew Henry: accosted by thieves and
robbed of his wallet...wrote in his diary: "Let me be
thankful first, because I was never robbed before;
second, because, although they took my wallet, they did
not take my life; third, although they took my all, it was
not much; and fourthly, because it was I who was
robbed, not I who robbed."

BE JOYFUL

Paul is not saying
"Be Happy Always"
but "BE JOYFUL
ALWAYS"

Does not depend on
circumstances...joy can
exist no matter what
happens...

"IN' all circumstances...NOT "because" of all
circumstances...We may not be thankful for something that has
happened...but we can be thankful that God is there to help us

Thinking more of
the Lord than of
Difficulties

It is easy to be pleasant
When life flows by like a song
But the person worth while is the
one who will smile
When everything goes dead wrong

GIVE THANKS
IN ALL
CIRCUMSTANCES

Write
"Give
Thanks" on
your TO DO
list

Write "Be
Joyful" on your
"TO DO" list

For the test of the heart is trouble
And it always comes with the years
And the smile that is worth the
praises of earth
Is the smile that shines through the
tears

In Vermont a farmer was sitting on the
porch with his wife. They had been married
42 years and he was finally beginning to
realize how much she meant to ghim. So he
turned to her and said, "Dear, You've been
such a wonderful woman that there are
times I can hardly keep from telling you."

CHRISTIAN TO
DO LIST
1Thess.5:16-18

CS Lewis: "Joy is never in our power, and pleasure is.
(But) I doubt whether anyone who has tasted Joy
would ever, if both were in his power, exchange is for
all the pleasure in the world/

Thankfulness should be a natural
response for us. Infortunately, we too
often take God's many gifts for granted
and forget to tell him thanks.

Reagan/Menachem Begin

USSR/USA

Political HQ

The attitude of prayerfulness can give us a
proper perspective on life because it keeps
us aware that we aren't alone as we
encounter the good and bad events of each
day. It keeps us aware of our dependence
on God. It keeps us aware that we are
always surrounded by God's love. This
knowledge we keep us always rejoicing.
Prayer and rejoicing are closely related, for
often the believer finds in prayer the means
of removing that which was the barrier to
his joy. Prayer is never just petition. Prayer
is fellowship with God. Prayer is the
realization of the presence of the Father.
We are to live in the spirit of prayer. (Paul's
example...often break into prayer)...**Having
an attitude of prayerfulness is living with
a continual consciousness of our
dependence on God and consciousness
of his presence.**

The Trio of injunctions
is completed with the
thought of continual
thanksgiving

God

"For this
is the will of God
for you in Christ
Jesus"

PRAYER is a local call

PRAY
CONTINUALLY

Write "Pray
Continually" on your
TO DO list

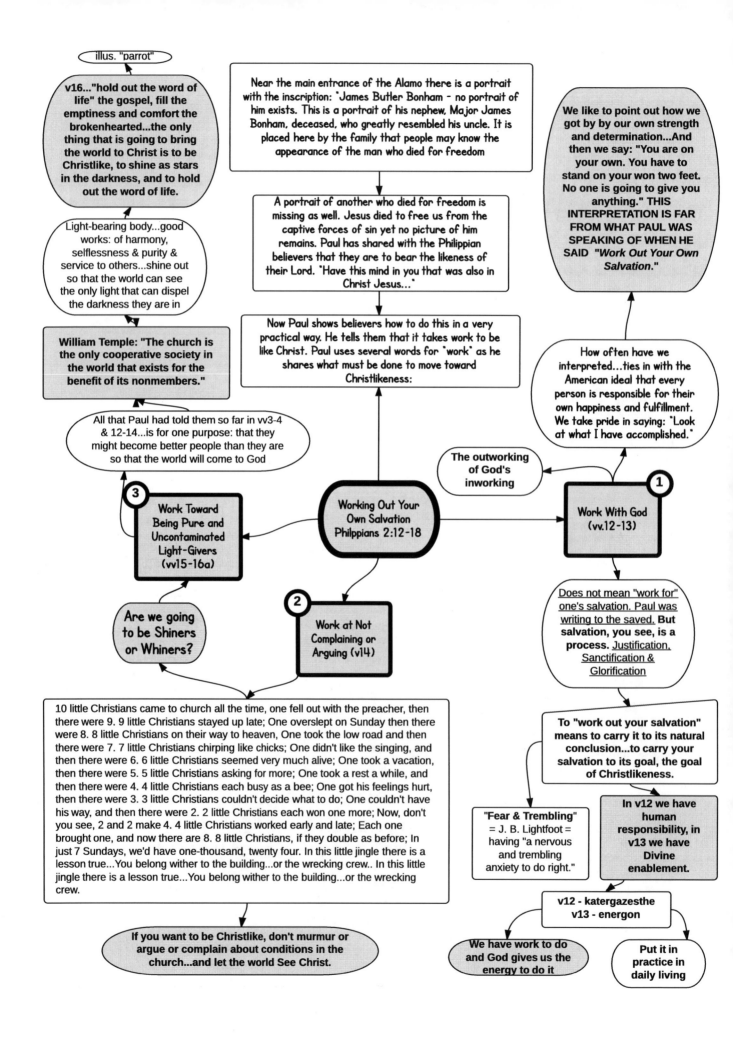

illus. "parrot"

v16..."hold out the word of life" the gospel, fill the emptiness and comfort the brokenhearted...the only thing that is going to bring the world to Christ is to be Christlike, to shine as stars in the darkness, and to hold out the word of life.

Near the main entrance of the Alamo there is a portrait with the inscription: "James Butler Bonham - no portrait of him exists. This is a portrait of his nephew, Major James Bonham, deceased, who greatly resembled his uncle. It is placed here by the family that people may know the appearance of the man who died for freedom

We like to point out how we got by by our own strength and determination...And then we say: "You are on your own. You have to stand on your won two feet. No one is going to give you anything." THIS INTERPRETATION IS FAR FROM WHAT PAUL WAS SPEAKING OF WHEN HE SAID "Work Out Your Own Salvation."

Light-bearing body...good works: of harmony, selflessness & purity & service to others...shine out so that the world can see the only light that can dispel the darkness they are in

A portrait of another who died for freedom is missing as well. Jesus died to free us from the captive forces of sin yet no picture of him remains. Paul has shared with the Philippian believers that they are to bear the likeness of their Lord. "Have this mind in you that was also in Christ Jesus..."

How often have we interpreted...ties in with the American ideal that every person is responsible for their own happiness and fulfillment. We take pride in saying: "Look at what I have accomplished."

William Temple: "The church is the only cooperative society in the world that exists for the benefit of its nonmembers."

Now Paul shows believers how to do this in a very practical way. He tells them that it takes work to be like Christ. Paul uses several words for "work" as he shares what must be done to move toward Christlikeness:

All that Paul had told them so far in vv3-4 & 12-14...is for one purpose: that they might become better people than they are so that the world will come to God

The outworking of God's inworking

3

Work Toward Being Pure and Uncontaminated Light-Givers (vv15-16a)

Working Out Your Own Salvation Philippians 2:12-18

1

Work With God (vv.12-13)

Are we going to be Shiners or Whiners?

2

Work at Not Complaining or Arguing (v14)

Does not mean "work for" one's salvation. Paul was writing to the saved. But salvation, you see, is a process. Justification, Sanctification & Glorification

10 little Christians came to church all the time, one fell out with the preacher, then there were 9. 9 little Christians stayed up late; One overslept on Sunday then there were 8. 8 little Christians on their way to heaven, One took the low road and then there were 7. 7 little Christians chirping like chicks; One didn't like the singing, and then there were 6. 6 little Christians seemed very much alive; One took a vacation, then there were 5. 5 little Christians asking for more; One took a rest a while, and then there were 4. 4 little Christians each busy as a bee; One got his feelings hurt, then there were 3. 3 little Christians couldn't decide what to do; One couldn't have his way, and then there were 2. 2 little Christians each won one more; Now, don't you see, 2 and 2 make 4. 4 little Christians worked early and late; Each one brought one, and now there are 8. 8 little Christians, if they double as before; In just 7 Sundays, we'd have one-thousand, twenty four. In this little jingle there is a lesson true...You belong wither to the building...or the wrecking crew.. In this little jingle there is a lesson true...You belong wither to the building...or the wrecking crew.

To "work out your salvation" means to carry it to its natural conclusion...to carry your salvation to its goal, the goal of Christlikeness.

"Fear & Trembling" = J. B. Lightfoot = having "a nervous and trembling anxiety to do right."

In v12 we have human responsibility, in v13 we have Divine enablement.

If you want to be Christlike, don't murmur or argue or complain about conditions in the church...and let the world See Christ.

v12 - katergazesthe v13 - energon

We have work to do and God gives us the energy to do it

Put it in practice in daily living

The comedian Jeff Foxworthy became famous with his routine, "You might be a redneck if . . . " Here are some of my favorites:
You might be a redneck if the directions to your house include the phrase "turn off the paved road".
You might be a redneck if your front porch collapses and four dogs get killed.
You might be a redneck if you took a fishing pole to Sea World.
You might be a redneck if you have to go outside to get something out of the 'fridge.
You might be a redneck if your dad walks you to school because you're both in the same grade.
You might be a redneck if you have flowers planted in a bathroom fixture in your front yard.
You might be a redneck if you think the last words to the Star Spangled Banner are, "Gentlemen, start your engines."
Likewise, you might be a Pharisee if you spend a more time talking about the sins of others than you do in repenting and confessing your own.

Sin is simply anything that takes our focus off of God → **Trust your Instruments**

Sin

Rom 3:23; 6:23

ἁμαρτία

Lie, Gossip, Slander, Greedy? Missed the Mark

Conclusion

1 Jn 1:9

All Sins are Serious...some are more Serious than others

Justice of God

Calvin: all sin is mortal in the sense that it rightly deserves death, but no sin is mortal in the sense that it destroys justifying grace.

Degrees of Sin John 19:1-11

Catholic

Mortal — Venial

Gal 5:19-21

At least 2 Degrees of Sin: forgivable & unforgivable

Key

Degrees of Sin?

John 19:11

Mt. 11:21-24 → Mk 12:38-40

1. The degree of one's guilt is relative to the degree of one's knowledge of truth

2. The degree of one's guilt is relative to the degree of one's intention involved in the sin

Unpardonable Sin Mt. 12:31-32

"Sin Unto Death" 1 Jn 5:16-17

physical death, although not eternal spiritual death

Lk 12:47-48

What it is...Xians? eternal/not conditional

Ananias and Sapphira in Acts 5:1-10, Corinth -LS

Num 15:27-28

unintentionally/presumptuously

Sins committed on purpose, with full consciousness of the evil involved, and with deliberation, are greater and more culpable than sins result-ing from ignorance, from an erroneous conception of things, or from weakness of character. Nevertheless the latter are also real sins and make one guilty in the sight of God.

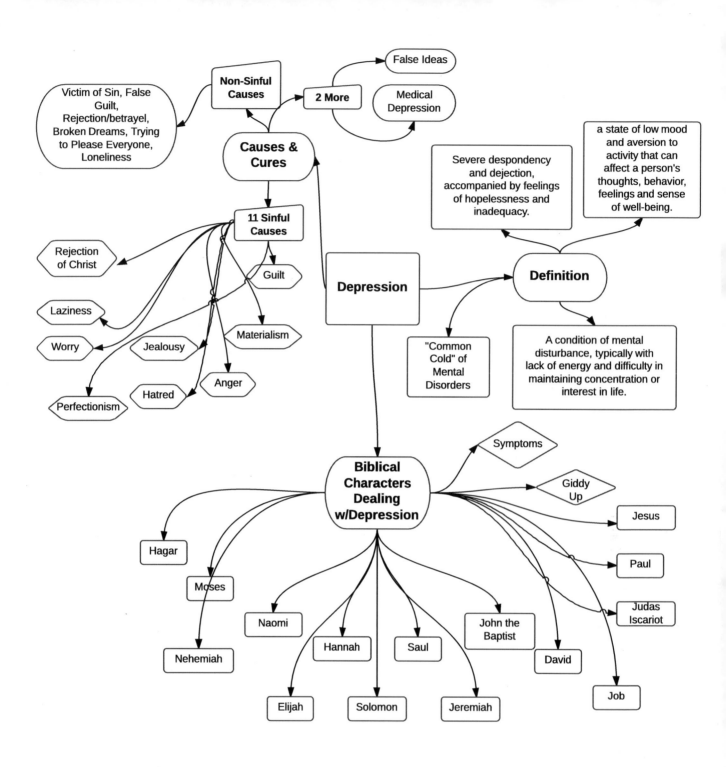

Non-Sinful Causes

Victim of Sin, False Guilt, Rejection/betrayel, Broken Dreams, Trying to Please Everyone, Loneliness

2 More

False Ideas

Medical Depression

Causes & Cures

11 Sinful Causes

Rejection of Christ

Laziness

Worry

Jealousy

Perfectionism

Hatred

Anger

Guilt

Materialism

Depression

Severe despondency and dejection, accompanied by feelings of hopelessness and inadequacy.

a state of low mood and aversion to activity that can affect a person's thoughts, behavior, feelings and sense of well-being.

Definition

"Common Cold" of Mental Disorders

A condition of mental disturbance, typically with lack of energy and difficulty in maintaining concentration or interest in life.

Biblical Characters Dealing w/Depression

Symptoms

Giddy Up

Jesus

Paul

Judas Iscariot

David

Job

Hagar

Moses

Nehemiah

Naomi

Hannah

Saul

John the Baptist

Elijah

Solomon

Jeremiah

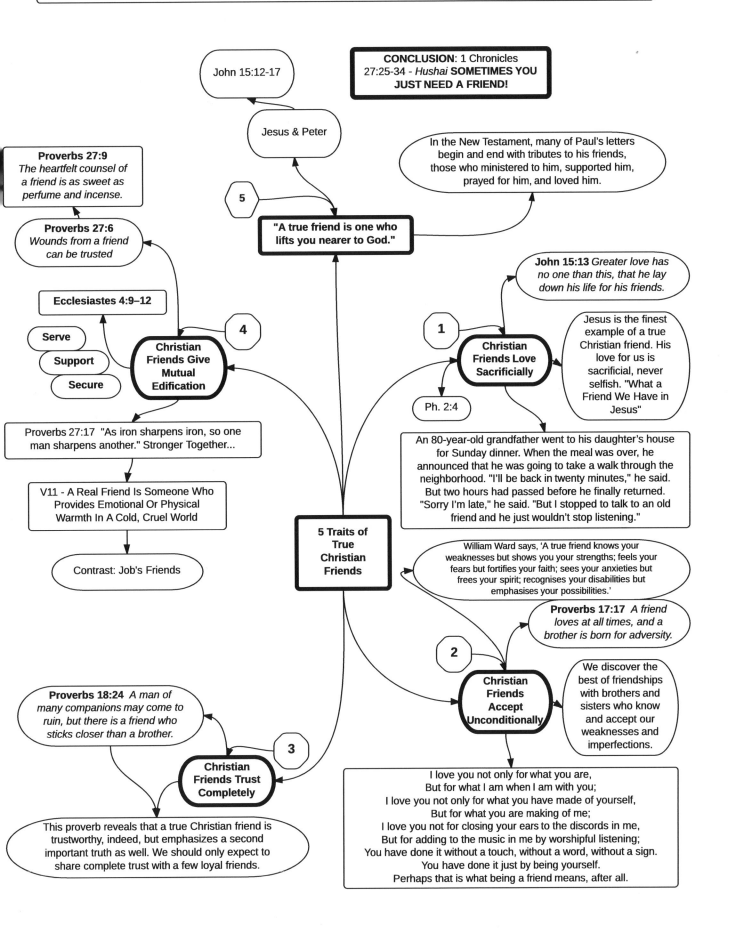

INTRODUCTION: In a survey of more than 40,000, Americans said these qualities were most valued in a friend: 1. The ability to keep confidences 2. Loyalty 3. Warmth and affection.

John 15:12-17

CONCLUSION: 1 Chronicles 27:25-34 - *Hushai* SOMETIMES YOU JUST NEED A FRIEND!

Jesus & Peter

In the New Testament, many of Paul's letters begin and end with tributes to his friends, those who ministered to him, supported him, prayed for him, and loved him.

Proverbs 27:9
The heartfelt counsel of a friend is as sweet as perfume and incense.

Proverbs 27:6
Wounds from a friend can be trusted

5

"A true friend is one who lifts you nearer to God."

John 15:13 *Greater love has no one than this, that he lay down his life for his friends.*

Ecclesiastes 4:9–12

4

Serve

Support

Secure

Christian Friends Give Mutual Edification

1

Christian Friends Love Sacrificially

Jesus is the finest example of a true Christian friend. His love for us is sacrificial, never selfish. "What a Friend We Have in Jesus"

Ph. 2:4

Proverbs 27:17 "As iron sharpens iron, so one man sharpens another." Stronger Together...

An 80-year-old grandfather went to his daughter's house for Sunday dinner. When the meal was over, he announced that he was going to take a walk through the neighborhood. "I'll be back in twenty minutes," he said. But two hours had passed before he finally returned. "Sorry I'm late," he said. "But I stopped to talk to an old friend and he just wouldn't stop listening."

V11 - A Real Friend Is Someone Who Provides Emotional Or Physical Warmth In A Cold, Cruel World

5 Traits of True Christian Friends

William Ward says, 'A true friend knows your weaknesses but shows you your strengths; feels your fears but fortifies your faith; sees your anxieties but frees your spirit; recognises your disabilities but emphasises your possibilities.'

Contrast: Job's Friends

Proverbs 17:17 *A friend loves at all times, and a brother is born for adversity.*

2

Christian Friends Accept Unconditionally

We discover the best of friendships with brothers and sisters who know and accept our weaknesses and imperfections.

Proverbs 18:24 *A man of many companions may come to ruin, but there is a friend who sticks closer than a brother.*

3

Christian Friends Trust Completely

This proverb reveals that a true Christian friend is trustworthy, indeed, but emphasizes a second important truth as well. We should only expect to share complete trust with a few loyal friends.

I love you not only for what you are,
But for what I am when I am with you;
I love you not only for what you have made of yourself,
But for what you are making of me;
I love you not for closing your ears to the discords in me,
But for adding to the music in me by worshipful listening;
You have done it without a touch, without a word, without a sign.
You have done it just by being yourself.
Perhaps that is what being a friend means, after all.

Spirit: Grows fruit that we find in the life of Christ

"You ♥ can keep the quarter, I done it for love."

"FRUIT" - sIngular

Story recorded in John 13: John begins the story with the words - *It was just before the Passover. ...he now showed them the full extent of his love.*

WHAT ALL OF THIS MEANS:

1. Our love flows from the knowledge of being loved by God.

2. We are to seek to show love in unselfish ways...wash dirt...

3. We must follow Christ's example to "Love to the Limit" in practical ways.

4. *Now that you know these things, you will be blessed if you do them.*

That radical thing about Jesus was that he was willing to do anything to show his love

LIVE THE FRUIT OF THE SPIRIT

WHAT VERSE 3 TELLS US:
1.Jesus knew the Father had given all things into his hands
2.Jesus knew that God was with him
3.Jesus knew who he as in relationship with the Father (coming/returning)

WHAT VERSES 12-17 TELL US - *When he had finished washing their feet, he put on his clothes and returned to his place. "Do you understand what I have done for you?" he asked them. 13 "You call me 'Teacher' and 'Lord,' and rightly so, for that is what I am. 14 Now that I, your Lord and Teacher, have washed your feet, you also should wash one another's feet. 15 I have set you an example that you should do as I have done for you. 16 I tell you the truth, no servant is greater than his master, nor is a messenger greater than the one who sent him. 17 Now that you know these things, you will be blessed if you do them.*

WHAT JESUS KNEW (V3)

WHAT JESUS SAID (V12-17)

WHAT V3 TEACHES US:
1.What Jesus knew helped to determine what he did...it set the **ATMOSPHERE** and the **ATTITUDE**
2.Love takes into account who we are and where we stand in relationship with God
3.Love take into account God's love for us

FRUIT OF THE SPIRIT: LOVE JOHN 13:1-17, 34-35

WHAT THESE VERSES TEACH US:

1. It was pure love that caused Jesus to do...
2. Jesus is our Source/Inspiration/Pattern...
3. We are to "Love to the Limit" (v1)

WHAT JESUS DID (V4-5)

PRIDE & DIRT : LESSONS THAT CAME FROM HIS ACTIONS

LESSON #1 - LOVE IS NOT SELFISH - letter

Dear Jimmy,
No words could express the great unhappiness I've fe;t since breaking our engagement. Please say you'll take me back. No one could ever take your place in my heart, so please forgive me. I love you, I love you, I love you! Yours forever, Marie
PS. And congratulations on winning the state lottery
LOVE doesn't ask "What's in it for me?" LOVE seeks to GIVE...not to GET...
CHAD - VALENTINES: "Not a one...not a one" And then added "I didn't forget a one...not a single one."

WHAT VERSES 4 & 5 TELL US:
1.The Master became the slave
2. The Highest took the place of the lowest
3.He took upon himself the duty of washing feet...
WHAT THESE VERSES TEACH US:
There are 2 reasons why Jesus chose to do this -
1.Their Hearts were Proud - ready to fight for a throne but not a towel...competative spirit...within a few minutes, arguing over who was greatest (Luke 22:24-30)! He gave them an unforgettable lesson in humility, and rebuked their selfishness and pride.
2.Their Feet were Dirty - The roads of palestine were unsurfaced and unclean. In dry weather they were dusty, in wet weather they were muddy. For that reason there were waterpots at the door of the house; and a servant was there with a towel to wash the soiled feet of the guests as they entered the house.

LESSON #2 - LOVE WASHES AWAY THE DIRT - Love doesn't throw dirt or expose dirt...it washes it away. ILLUS. Cowboy first time in church: corral, main gate, long chute, box stalls/pew "That's what the lady said when I sat down beside her." (1) love doesn't point out the dirt on others...love seeks to bring God's cleansing to others. (2) Love seeks to help clean up other's messes (3) Love even washes the feet of Judas

Mt 3:8 - *Produce fruit in keeping with repentance.*

LIVE THE FRUIT OF THE SPIRIT

Jn. 15:16 - *You did not choose me, but I chose you and appointed you to go and bear fruit--fruit that will last. Then the Father will give you whatever you ask in my name.*

fruitfulness

(1) **Contact with Living Water** - *He is like a tree planted by streams of water, which yields its fruit in season and whose leaf does not wither. Whatever he does prospers. - Ps 1:3*

Ro. 7:4 - *So, my brothers, you also died to the law through the body of Christ, that you might belong to another, to him who was raised from the dead, in order that we might bear fruit to God.*

Col. 1:10 - *And we pray this in order that you may live a life worthy of the Lord and may please him in every way: bearing fruit in every good work, growing in the knowledge of God*

(2) **Spiritual Receptivity** - *But the one who received the seed that fell on good soil is the man who hears the word and understands it. He produces a crop, yielding a hundred, sixty or thirty times what was sown." - Mt 13:23*

Conditions for Fruitbearing

Fruit of the Spirit Introduction

Fruitfulness & Unfruitfulness

(3) **Death of the Old Life** - *I tell you the truth, unless a kernel of wheat falls to the ground and dies, it remains only a single seed. But if it dies, it produces many seeds. - Jn 12:24*

Mt. 3:10 - *The ax is already at the root of the trees, and every tree that does not produce good fruit will be cut down and thrown into the fire.*

(4) **Death of the Old Life** - *He cuts off every branch in me that bears no fruit, while every branch that does bear fruit he prunes so that it will be even more fruitful. - Jn 15:2*

Not dependant on Age

Unfruitfulness

Ps 92:12-14 - *The righteous will flourish like a palm tree, they will grow like a cedar of Lebanon; planted in the house of the LORD, they will flourish in the courts of our God. They will still bear fruit in old age, they will stay fresh and green*

Mt. 13:22 - *The one who received the seed that fell among the thorns is the man who hears the word, but the worries of this life and the deceitfulness of wealth choke it, making it unfruitful.*

(5) **Abiding in Christ** - *"I am the vine; you are the branches. If a man remains in me and I in him, he will bear much fruit; apart from me you can do nothing. - Jn 15:5*

CONCLUSION: The simplest meaning of Easter is that we are living in a world in which God has the last word. And that word is "You have not been forsaken. You have been forgiven. There is grace for the guilty...and your future is wide open!"

And what a future he had with his Lord...

Listen to Peter's own words expressing what the resurrection meant to him. 1 Peter 1:3-5

Why single out Peter?

Mark - significant

DENIAL

Peter didn't think he would ever be able to live free from regret and guilt

Warning about self-confidence

CAN YOU RELATE TO PETER?

The last time he saw his Lord was...

unanimous

Regrets/Do Overs

Someone once said: "If at first you don't succeed...make sure that you cover up all evidence that you even tried." But the evidence is difficult to cover up.

Peter need to know he had a FUTURE with Jesus

Peter needed to know he was not FORSAKEN

"TELL PETER"...JESUS WANTED PETER TO KNOW THAT TO FAIL DOESN'T MAKE ONE A FAILURE. WHAT HAPPENED IN THE COURTYARD DOESN'T END THE RELATIONSHIP PETER HAS WITH JESUS. GOD'S LOVE REACHES OUT TO THOSE WHO HAVE FAILED.

E. Stanley Jones' friend...turned to the NT as the original source and example of how Jesus conducted a funeral. And he found that Jesus didn't conduct funerals at all. All he dealt with were resurrections. **All Jesus deals with are NEW BEGINNINGS.**

He **FAILED** but he was not forgotten

Shame over past failures & sins can haunt and inhibit us in many ways. Satan likes to keep our failures in front of us. But Jesus intends to redeem us completely.

Life tells us "It's too late!" We can't begin again. There is too much water under the bridge...But with God...

Go and Tell Peter Mark 16:1-7

Beautiful chorus in our hymnal written by Mark Blankenship:
It is simply entitled: "Forgiven."
Forgiven, I've been forgiven;
God has looked beyond my sin,
Saved me from what I might have been,
Gave me a new life within,
I am forgiven by His Grace.

This is what Peter needed to hear.........! The denial of Christ....failure to live up to his own expectations...

King Louis XII of France...his enemies...names on a scroll with a cross in red ink behind each name. "The cross which I drew beside each name was not a sign of punishment, but a pledge of forgiveness extended for the sake of the crucified Savior, who upon his cross forgave his enemies and prayed for them."

Peter needed to know he was FORGIVEN

Dwight Moody: "The voice of sin is **LOUD,** but the voice of forgiveness is **LOUDER!**

If we had the Wisdom of Solomon, the Patience of John, the Meekness of Moses, the Strength of Samson, the Obedience of Abraham, the Compassion of Joseph, the Tears of Jeremiah, the Poetic Skill of David, the Prophetic Voice of Elijah, the Courage of Daniel, the Greatness of John the Baptist, the Endurance and Love of Paul, **WE WOULD STILL NEED REDEMPTION THROUGH CHRIST'S BLOOD. THE FORGIVENESS OF SIN** (R.L.Wheeler)

I've fallen in love with the GPS in my car. It never gets annoyed at me. If I make a mistake, it says, "Recalculating." And then it tells me to make the soonest left turn and go back. I thought to myself, you know, I should write a book and call it "Recalculating" because I think that that's what we're doing all the time. So this is an example of technology instilling us with spiritual discipline, And no matter how many times I don't make that turn, it will continue to say, "Recalculating." The tone of voice will stay the same. IT doesn't say: "You dummy..." WE need to know how to find the Way...Scripture gives us the directions we need. But the key is knowing that JESUS is the WAY!

how about this case: I am not making this up; it really happened! First, the criminal was as guilty as sin. There was no doubt about it. Second, the judge correctly decides on the appropriate sentence based upon what the many crimes deserved. The sentence was death. So here we have a felon on death row who deserves to die. There does not seem to be a whole lot wrong with that. Everything is pretty much as it should be. But wait. The judge has a tender spot for the felon. You see, the felon is also the judge's son! The son bears a distinct family resemblance, and though his crimes have caused the judge great sorrow, the judge still loves his son. So, guess what. Even while the son has yet to show any remorse, the judge devises a rather complicated plan whereby the wayward son can live. He allows someone else, one who is not guilty, to step in and pay the penalty for the guilty, and then declares to the guilty, "You're free to go. I hope this all means something to you and will cause you to think seriously about changing the course of your life, to come back home and start over." Yes, it is a true story! God is the Judge and Father, Jesus is the substitute, and the guilty son; well, Th... that, uh...that would be me.

v17 - "blessed" - makarios = happy, fortunate

4 The Way to Happiness John 13:15-17

1 The Way to Pardon Acts 13:38-39a

Micah 7:18

must be accepted

1. Cultivate Gratitude 2. Foster Forgiveness
3. Practice Prayer 4. Foster Christian Friendship
- There are few better antidotes to unhappiness than close friendships with people who care about you, says David G. Myers, author of The Pursuit of Happiness. One Australian study found that people over 70 who had the strongest network of friends lived much longer.

In the early 1800's, President Andrew Jackson offered a pardon to a man named George Wilson (no, not Dennis Mitchell's next door neighbor) who had been sentenced to death by hanging. Mr. Wilson refused the pardon. Supreme Court justice John Marshall declared, "the value of the pardon depends upon its acceptance. If it is refused, then there is no pardon." Mr. Mitchell died on the gallows.

Jesus is the Way John 14:6 Part 1

"The Lord will perfect that which concerns me; Your mercy, O Lord, endures forever" (Ps. 138:8). Whatever time it takes, He is committed to your completion, and that completed work will be a work of holiness unto the Lord

Nehemiah 9:17 KJV

Customer to waitress: How do you prepare your chicken?" Waitress: "We tell them straight up they're not going to make it"

katharos = pure, clean, innocent

But if we walk in the light, as he is in the light, we have fellowship with one another, and the blood of Jesus, his Son, _purifies_ us from every sin.

Therefore, since we have been justified through faith, we have peace with God through our Lord Jesus Christ

What God does in us

3 The Way to Holiness 1 John 1:7

2 The Way to Peace Romans 5:1-5

Fact not Feeling...

Catharsis Psychiatry.

discharge of pent-up emotions so as to result in the alleviation of symptoms or the permanent relief of the condition.

"Be holy as I am holy" Holiness—His holy nature—is progressively going to fill my broken, weak and damaged parts. The character and constancy of my Father will grow in me.

Comparing Peace

"of God" & "with God"

World's Peace
1. Dependent on feelings
2. Must be seen
3. Does not allow for troubles
4. Feels must manage situation
5. Tries to control
6. Ultimately fails

versus

God's Peace
1. Dependent on trust
2. No need to be seen
3. Allows for troubles
4. Need not manage situation
5. Trust God to control
6. Always endures

Do you want a peace that fails you just when you need it the most?

Do you desire a peace that keeps you calm in the most threatening situations?

The word in some form—holy, holiness, holiest, allow, hallowed—occurs nearly 700 times in the English Bible. Certainly, it's an important word. The average believer seems to feel threatened by the idea of holiness. He tends to see it as something unapproachable, a demanding standard of life that seems to be well beyond him. Believers tend to define it by "feel" more than by fact, and the feeling seems to be, "Boy, that's way beyond me (although I sure want to try my best!)."

TO TELL THE TRUTH: The show features a panel of four celebrities whose object is the correct identification of a described contestant who has an unusual occupation or experience. This central character is accompanied by two impostors who pretend to be the central character; together, the three persons are said to belong to a "team of challengers." The celebrity panelists question the three contestants; the impostors are allowed to lie but the central character is sworn "to tell the truth". After questioning, the panel attempts to identify which of the three challengers is telling the truth and is thus the central character.

Truth is far more than facts. It's not just something we act upon. It acts upon us. We can't change the truth, but the truth can change us. It sanctifies (sets us apart) from the falsehoods

This is what separates Jesus Christ from every other leader of every other faith. Other leaders have said, "I'm looking for the truth" or "I'm teaching the truth" or "I point to the truth" or "I'm a prophet of truth." Jesus comes and says, "I am the truth."

Luke 15:11-24
He is Father

John 3:16-17

The Truth about Faith

TRUTH IS A PERSON

The Truth about God

Faith grows

mustard seed

Faith in God

Faith brings results

Yes

Yes

Mt. 17:20-21

1 Jn. 4:4 - Faith in God's Power

Forgiving

Grace

Just

Love

Sovereign

A grandfather found his grandson, jumping up and down in his playpen, crying at the top of his voice. When Johnnie saw his grandfather, he reached up his little chubby hands and said, "Out, Gramp, out."
It was only natural for Grandfather to reach down to lift the little fellow out of his predicament; but as he did, the mother of the child stepped up and said, "No, Johnnie, you are being punished, so you must stay in."
The grandfather was at a loss to know what to do. The child's tears and chubby hands reached deep into his heart, but the mother's firmness in correcting her son for misbehavior must not be lightly taken. Here was a problem of love versus law, but love found a way. The grandfather could not take the youngster out of the playpen, so he crawled in with him.
God did not spare Paul and Silas the suffering and imprisonment, but He did come down into the prison with them.
God did not keep the three Hebrew children out of the fiery furnace, but He went into the furnace with them.
God will not always deliver us from trouble and heartache, but He has promised grace for every situation of life.

Jesus is the TRUTH
John 14:6
Part 2

During a trial, in a small Missouri town, the local prosecuting attorney called his first witness to the stand. The witness was a proper well-dressed elderly lady, the Grandmother type, well spoken, and poised. She was sworn in, asked if she would tell the truth, the whole truth and nothing but the truth, on the Bible, so help her God.
The prosecuting attorney approached the woman and asked, "Mrs. Jones, do you know me?'" She responded, "Why, yes I do know you, Mr. Williams. I've known you since you were a young boy and frankly, you've been a big disappointment to me. You lie, cheat on your wife, manipulate people and talk badly about them behind their backs. You think you're a rising big shot when you haven't the sense to realize you never will amount to anything more than a two-bit paper-pushing shyster. Yes, I know you quite well."
The lawyer was stunned. Not knowing what else to do, he pointed across the room and asked, "Mrs. Jones, do you know the defense attorney?"
She again replied, "Why, yes, I do. I've known Mr. Bradley since he was a youngster, too. He's lazy, bigoted, has a bad drinking problem. The man can't build or keep a normal relationship with anyone and his law practice is one of the worst in the entire state. Not to mention he cheated on his wife with three different women. Yes, I know him."
The defense attorney almost fainted. Laughter mixed with gasps, thundered throughout the courtroom and the audience was on the verge of chaos.
At this point, the judge brought the courtroom to silence, called both counselors to the bench, and in a very quiet voice said, "If either of you morons asks her if she knows me, you're going to jail."

John 13:34

The Truth about Love

Matt. 22:37-40

Yes

The Truth about Man

love enemies

A cost to love

Love God

Love & obedience

love neighbor

Yes

Lost

Like sheep

Spiritually sick

man must prioritize

man is sinful

needs salvation

Yes

Jn. 14:23

Parent/teen - unconditional love

As followers of Christ, we are to walk in the truth (3 John 1:3), love the truth, and believe the truth (2 Thessalonians 2:10-12). We're to speak the truth "in love" (Ephesians 4:32).

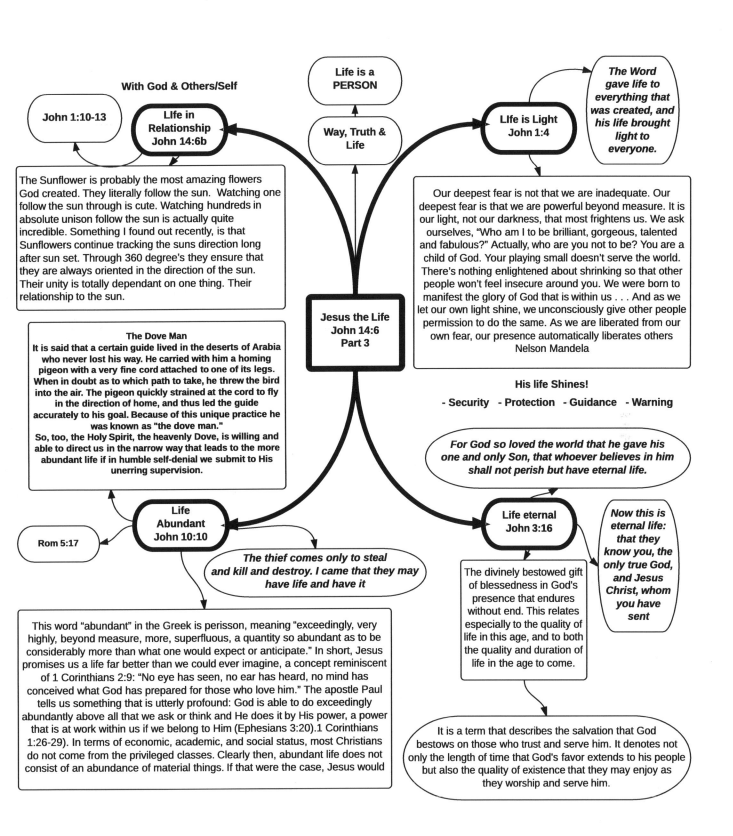

With God & Others/Self

Life is a PERSON

Way, Truth & Life

Life is Light
John 1:4

The Word gave life to everything that was created, and his life brought light to everyone.

John 1:10-13

LIfe in Relationship
John 14:6b

The Sunflower is probably the most amazing flowers God created. They literally follow the sun. Watching one follow the sun through is cute. Watching hundreds in absolute unison follow the sun is actually quite incredible. Something I found out recently, is that Sunflowers continue tracking the suns direction long after sun set. Through 360 degree's they ensure that they are always oriented in the direction of the sun. Their unity is totally dependant on one thing. Their relationship to the sun.

Our deepest fear is not that we are inadequate. Our deepest fear is that we are powerful beyond measure. It is our light, not our darkness, that most frightens us. We ask ourselves, "Who am I to be brilliant, gorgeous, talented and fabulous?" Actually, who are you not to be? You are a child of God. Your playing small doesn't serve the world. There's nothing enlightened about shrinking so that other people won't feel insecure around you. We were born to manifest the glory of God that is within us . . . And as we let our own light shine, we unconsciously give other people permission to do the same. As we are liberated from our own fear, our presence automatically liberates others
Nelson Mandela

The Dove Man
It is said that a certain guide lived in the deserts of Arabia who never lost his way. He carried with him a homing pigeon with a very fine cord attached to one of its legs. When in doubt as to which path to take, he threw the bird into the air. The pigeon quickly strained at the cord to fly in the direction of home, and thus led the guide accurately to his goal. Because of this unique practice he was known as "the dove man."
So, too, the Holy Spirit, the heavenly Dove, is willing and able to direct us in the narrow way that leads to the more abundant life if in humble self-denial we submit to His unerring supervision.

Jesus the Life
John 14:6
Part 3

His life Shines!

- Security   - Protection   - Guidance   - Warning

For God so loved the world that he gave his one and only Son, that whoever believes in him shall not perish but have eternal life.

Life Abundant
John 10:10

Rom 5:17

The thief comes only to steal and kill and destroy. I came that they may have life and have it

Life eternal
John 3:16

Now this is eternal life: that they know you, the only true God, and Jesus Christ, whom you have sent

The divinely bestowed gift of blessedness in God's presence that endures without end. This relates especially to the quality of life in this age, and to both the quality and duration of life in the age to come.

This word "abundant" in the Greek is perisson, meaning "exceedingly, very highly, beyond measure, more, superfluous, a quantity so abundant as to be considerably more than what one would expect or anticipate." In short, Jesus promises us a life far better than we could ever imagine, a concept reminiscent of 1 Corinthians 2:9: "No eye has seen, no ear has heard, no mind has conceived what God has prepared for those who love him." The apostle Paul tells us something that is utterly profound: God is able to do exceedingly abundantly above all that we ask or think and He does it by His power, a power that is at work within us if we belong to Him (Ephesians 3:20).1 Corinthians 1:26-29). In terms of economic, academic, and social status, most Christians do not come from the privileged classes. Clearly then, abundant life does not consist of an abundance of material things. If that were the case, Jesus would

It is a term that describes the salvation that God bestows on those who trust and serve him. It denotes not only the length of time that God's favor extends to his people but also the quality of existence that they may enjoy as they worship and serve him.

A man was spending his holiday in Africa. One day he watched the elephants passing by. To his great surprise these giant strong animals were being held only by a small rope, tied to their front leg. Obviously, they could easily run away any moment. However, they did not. Then he saw a trainer and asked him, how could this happen that not a single elephant makes an attempt to break free. The trainer explained: „When the elephants are very young, we use the same size rope to tie them, and at that time it is enough to hold them. Gradually they grow up, get stronger, nevertheless they never try to get away, as they believe that the rope will still hold them. The man was stunned. These strong animals could break free any time, but they did not, because they believed that this is impossible. Sometimes people act like elephants, when they give up after the first failure. Remember, that failures are part of learning. If we want to succeed, we should never give up, but try and try again.

Webster's: Judgment = "*The process of forming an opinion or evaluation by discerning and comparing; an opinion or estimate so formed; the capacity for judging; discernment, the exercise of this capacity; a proposition stating something believed or asserted*"

The fact is, we use judgment everyday in the decision-making process...Who gets to decide if you are showing good judgment? Who do you listen to?

Sovereignty of God

The belief that God controls everything that happens to us is one of the devil's biggest inroads into our lives. If this belief is true, then our actions are irrelevant, and our efforts are meaningless. What will be will be...in the long-term, it slanders God, hinders our trust in God

4

Rev. 2-3

Never Give Up

Heb. 12:1-3

1

Make the Decision to Let God Be God

You'll never make progress as long as you refuse to give up control.

Prov. 16:1-3

Control-freak

Be glad about your progress. Let yourself off the hook. You didn't start showing poor judgment overnight & you won't always show good judgment now, just because you want to. Just be happy you're making progress and you're seeing your life improve. Little by little as you gain wisdom from God's word, you'll begin to see the results reflected in your decisions.

4 Keys to Making the Right Decisions

2 Peter 3:9

Matthew 7:13

There is someone more qualified than me in charge of my life

The answer comes when you look to God for a solution. Believing and relying on God's word will shed an incredible light on just about any issue. God has a plan for all of our lives and our days. So when you work with God, he gives you the GRACE to make right decisions and show good judgment.

3

Surround Yourself with People Who are Further Along in the Journey

2

Study the Word of God

2 Tim. 2:15

1 Cor 11:1

There is no reason to learn every lesson yourself when you have perfectly good examples right in front of you. Take advantage of counsel.

"You will do foolish things, but do them with enthusiasm."

"Admit your errors before someone else exaggerates them." ~ Andrew V. Mason

Biblical principles should inform our decisions. The Bible & Decision-Making:
1. Proverbs 3:5-7
2. Proverbs 18:13
3. Proverbs 21:5
4. Proverbs 17:10
5. Proverbs 11:14
6. Proverbs 10:17
7. Proverbs 14:15

2 Cor. 1:3-5

You can take comfort in knowing that one day your mistakes may serve to help someone else.

"As long as the world is turning and spinning, we're gonna be dizzy and we're gonna make mistakes." ~ Mel Brooks

CONCLUSION: HOW DO WE MAKE GOD PERSONAL?
1. Realize the He is a Personal God
2. Become Personal with the Personal God... "God," says Emerson, "enters into every life by a private door." It is all Personal. Can you say:
The Lord is MY LIGHT?
The Lord is MY SALVATION?
The Lord is MY SECURITY?

God wants us to know him.
The Bible says God is at work in everyone's life. "*So that they should seek the Lord, in the hope that they might grope for Him and find Him, though He is not far from each one of us.*"
(Acts 17:27)

When we make God Personal, our fears are calmed: - 700 phobias...even Phobophoboa = the fear of fear. When Saddam Hussein was in power...had doubles, never slept in same bed twice, slept in van on side of road...everyone, even relatives and friends were strip searched. 100's wanted to kill him. Lived everyday in fear...

READ V. 3

I need a stronghold! I need to feel secure as I face life. So do you! "The Lord is my Strongold"

David... "Stronghold/ Safety.... read v. 5

Golden Gate Bridge...23 fell to death...net...10 fell...25% more work...Because assurance of safety...

In <u>Executive Edge</u>, management consultant Ken Blanchard...They saw little Schia walk quietly up to her baby brother, put her face close to his, and say, "Baby, tell me what God feels like. I'm starting to forget." DON'T WE FORGET SOMETIMES? DON'T WE NEED TO BE REMINDED?

The Scriptures teach us that God is Lord over all...Ps. 24:1 Jesus taught his disciples to pray "Our Father". The Lod above all is over all. He is "The" God and He is "Our" God. All of these statements are right and true. But there must come a time when "The" Lord becomea "My" Lord..."The" God, "My" God

The life of Christianity consists of possessive pronouns," say Martin Luther. It is one thing to say "Christ is a Savior", it is quite another thing to say "He is my Savior and Lord". The devil can say the first; the true Christian alone can say the second."

Psalm 27:1 reminds us of this...My Light...My Salvation...My Security/Stronghold. He rules nations and governs nature...but he also provides for my personal needs: Light...Salvation...Security:

My, My, My...A Personal God Ps. 27:1, 4-9

Glow in the dark Volleyball

1 LIght
Light is important. Light helps us see the road ahead. Light takes away the fear of the darkness of the unknown. Light helps us to see ourselves better.

Isaiah 60:1, 19-20 John 1:4-5

"The Lord is My Light" **I NEED LIGHT!** I need a lighted path to walk. So do you! **THE LORD IS MY LIGHT!**

3 SECURITY

2 Salvation

Salvation From/For

E. Peterson: "We can't save ourselves by pulling on our bootstraps, even when the bootstraps are made of the finest religious leather."

An old Indian chief constantly spoke of Jesus and what e meant to him. "Why do you talk so much about Jesus?" asked a friend. caterpillar...circle of fie..."My help can only come from above." ...extended his finger...crawle to safety..."That was what Jesus did for me"................David sais "The Lord is My Salvation." He saves ne from a life controlled by self and sin. "My Savior"

I NEED SALVATION! I NEED TO BE SAVED FROM MY PAST...FROM MY GUILT...FROM MYSELF! SO DO YOU. "THE LORD IS MY SALVATION."

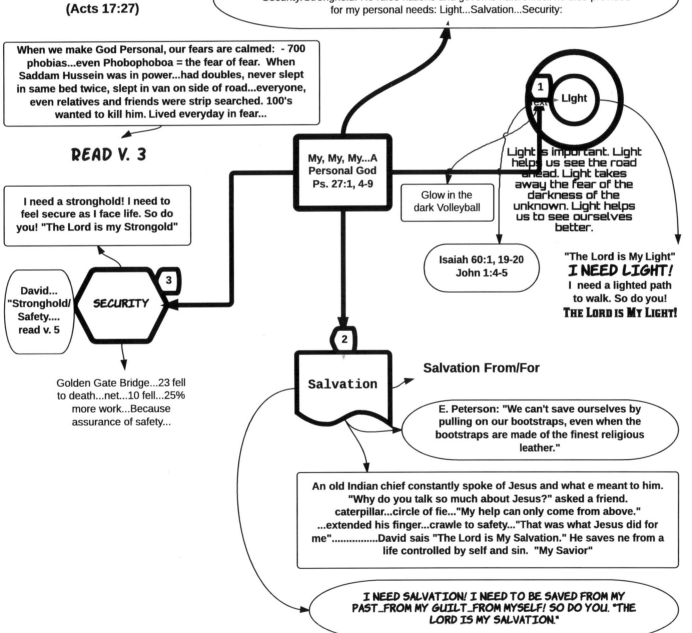

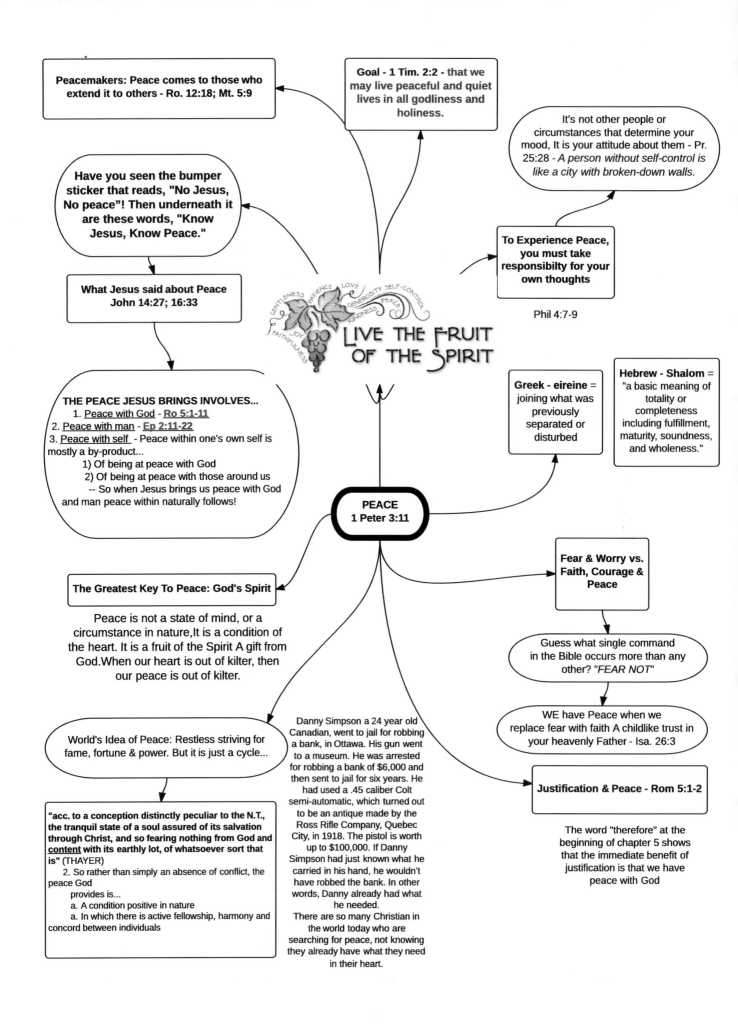

Peacemakers: Peace comes to those who extend it to others - Ro. 12:18; Mt. 5:9

Goal - 1 Tim. 2:2 - that we may live peaceful and quiet lives in all godliness and holiness.

It's not other people or circumstances that determine your mood, It is your attitude about them - Pr. 25:28 - *A person without self-control is like a city with broken-down walls.*

Have you seen the bumper sticker that reads, "No Jesus, No peace"! Then underneath it are these words, "Know Jesus, Know Peace."

To Experience Peace, you must take responsibilty for your own thoughts

Phil 4:7-9

What Jesus said about Peace John 14:27; 16:33

LIVE THE FRUIT OF THE SPIRIT

GENTLENESS PATIENCE LOVE GENEROSITY SELF-CONTROL KINDNESS PEACE JOY FAITHFULNESS

Greek - eireine = joining what was previously separated or disturbed

Hebrew - Shalom = "a basic meaning of totality or completeness including fulfillment, maturity, soundness, and wholeness."

THE PEACE JESUS BRINGS INVOLVES...
1. Peace with God - Ro 5:1-11
2. Peace with man - Ep 2:11-22
3. Peace with self - Peace within one's own self is mostly a by-product...
1) Of being at peace with God
2) Of being at peace with those around us
-- So when Jesus brings us peace with God and man peace within naturally follows!

PEACE
1 Peter 3:11

Fear & Worry vs. Faith, Courage & Peace

The Greatest Key To Peace: God's Spirit

Peace is not a state of mind, or a circumstance in nature, It is a condition of the heart. It is a fruit of the Spirit A gift from God. When our heart is out of kilter, then our peace is out of kilter.

Guess what single command in the Bible occurs more than any other? "*FEAR NOT*"

WE have Peace when we replace fear with faith A childlike trust in your heavenly Father - Isa. 26:3

World's Idea of Peace: Restless striving for fame, fortune & power. But it is just a cycle...

Danny Simpson a 24 year old Canadian, went to jail for robbing a bank, in Ottawa. His gun went to a museum. He was arrested for robbing a bank of $6,000 and then sent to jail for six years. He had used a .45 caliber Colt semi-automatic, which turned out to be an antique made by the Ross Rifle Company, Quebec City, in 1918. The pistol is worth up to $100,000. If Danny Simpson had just known what he carried in his hand, he wouldn't have robbed the bank. In other words, Danny already had what he needed.
There are so many Christian in the world today who are searching for peace, not knowing they already have what they need in their heart.

Justification & Peace - Rom 5:1-2

The word "therefore" at the beginning of chapter 5 shows that the immediate benefit of justification is that we have peace with God

"acc. to a conception distinctly peculiar to the N.T., the tranquil state of a soul assured of its salvation through Christ, and so fearing nothing from God and content with its earthly lot, of whatsoever sort that is" (THAYER)
2. So rather than simply an absence of conflict, the peace God
   provides is...
   a. A condition positive in nature
   a. In which there is active fellowship, harmony and concord between individuals

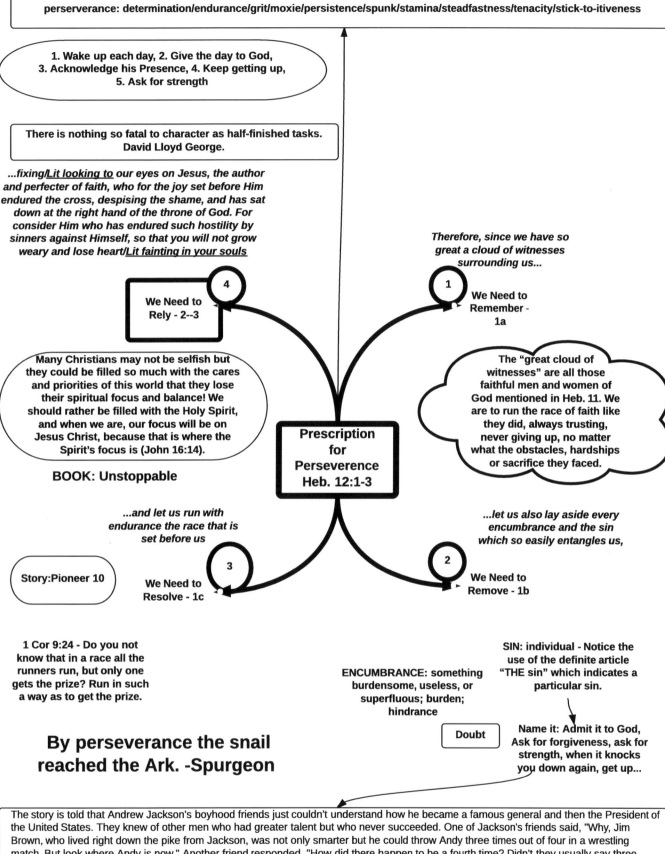

perserverance: determination/endurance/grit/moxie/persistence/spunk/stamina/steadfastness/tenacity/stick-to-itiveness

1. Wake up each day, 2. Give the day to God,
3. Acknowledge his Presence, 4. Keep getting up,
5. Ask for strength

There is nothing so fatal to character as half-finished tasks.
David Lloyd George.

...fixing/Lit looking to our eyes on Jesus, the author and perfecter of faith, who for the joy set before Him endured the cross, despising the shame, and has sat down at the right hand of the throne of God. For consider Him who has endured such hostility by sinners against Himself, so that you will not grow weary and lose heart/Lit fainting in your souls

Therefore, since we have so great a cloud of witnesses surrounding us...

4

We Need to
Rely - 2--3

1

We Need to
Remember -
1a

Many Christians may not be selfish but they could be filled so much with the cares and priorities of this world that they lose their spiritual focus and balance! We should rather be filled with the Holy Spirit, and when we are, our focus will be on Jesus Christ, because that is where the Spirit's focus is (John 16:14).

BOOK: Unstoppable

The "great cloud of witnesses" are all those faithful men and women of God mentioned in Heb. 11. We are to run the race of faith like they did, always trusting, never giving up, no matter what the obstacles, hardships or sacrifice they faced.

**Prescription
for
Perseverence
Heb. 12:1-3**

...and let us run with endurance the race that is set before us

...let us also lay aside every encumbrance and the sin which so easily entangles us,

Story:Pioneer 10

3

We Need to
Resolve - 1c

2

We Need to
Remove - 1b

1 Cor 9:24 - Do you not know that in a race all the runners run, but only one gets the prize? Run in such a way as to get the prize.

ENCUMBRANCE: something burdensome, useless, or superfluous; burden; hindrance

SIN: individual - Notice the use of the definite article "THE sin" which indicates a particular sin.

Doubt

Name it: Admit it to God, Ask for forgiveness, ask for strength, when it knocks you down again, get up...

By perseverance the snail reached the Ark. -Spurgeon

The story is told that Andrew Jackson's boyhood friends just couldn't understand how he became a famous general and then the President of the United States. They knew of other men who had greater talent but who never succeeded. One of Jackson's friends said, "Why, Jim Brown, who lived right down the pike from Jackson, was not only smarter but he could throw Andy three times out of four in a wrestling match. But look where Andy is now." Another friend responded, "How did there happen to be a fourth time? Didn't they usually say three times and out?" "Sure, they were supposed to, but not Andy. He would never admit he was beat -- he would never stay 'throwed.' Jim Brown would get tired, and on the fourth try Andrew Jackson would throw him and be the winner." Picking up on that idea, someone has said, "The thing that counts is not how many times you are 'throwed,' but whether you are willing to stay 'throwed'." We may face setbacks, but we must take courage and go forward in faith. Then, through the Holy Spirit's power we can be the eventual victor over sin and the world. The battle is the Lord's, so there is no excuse for us to stay "throwed"!

The acrostic form and the use of the Torah words constitute the framework for an elaborate prayer. The grounds for the prayer are established in the first two stanzas (alef and beth): the Torah is held up as a source of blessing and right conduct, and the psalmist pledges to dedicate himself to the law.

PSALM 119

Longest Psalm

Yes

176 verses

The name of God (Yahweh) appears twenty-four times.

Author Unknown

22 stanzas of 8 lines each. Each eight line stanza begins with same letter of Hebrew alphabet

There is a tradition in the Eastern Orthodox Church that King David used this psalm to teach his son Solomon both the Hebrew alphabet and the "alphabet of the spiritual life."

With its 176 verses, Psalm 119 has more verses than 14 Old Testament Books and 17 New Testament Books.

Use this Psalm as a tuning fork to tune your heart to love God's word more.

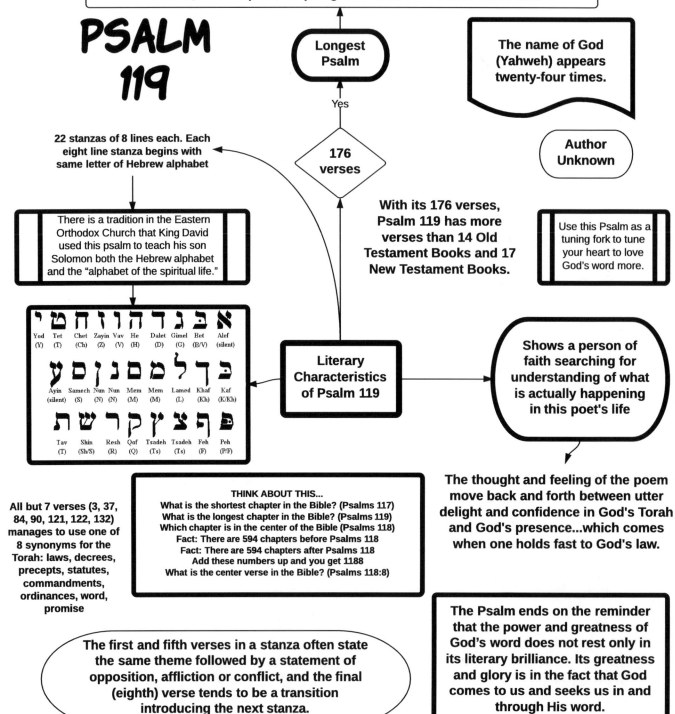

Yod (Y)	Tet (T)	Chet (Ch)	Zayin (Z)	Vav (V)	He (H)	Dalet (D)	Gimel (G)	Bet (B/V)	Alef (silent)
Ayin (silent)	Samech (S)	Nun (N)	Nun (N)	Mem (M)	Mem (M)	Lamed (L)	Khaf (Kh)	Kaf (K/Kh)	
Tav (T)	Shin (Sh/S)	Resh (R)	Qof (Q)	Tsadeh (Ts)	Tsadeh (Ts)	Feh (F)	Peh (P/F)		

Literary Characteristics of Psalm 119

Shows a person of faith searching for understanding of what is actually happening in this poet's life

The thought and feeling of the poem move back and forth between utter delight and confidence in God's Torah and God's presence...which comes when one holds fast to God's law.

All but 7 verses (3, 37, 84, 90, 121, 122, 132) manages to use one of 8 synonyms for the Torah: laws, decrees, precepts, statutes, commandments, ordinances, word, promise

THINK ABOUT THIS...
What is the shortest chapter in the Bible? (Psalms 117)
What is the longest chapter in the Bible? (Psalms 119)
Which chapter is in the center of the Bible (Psalms 118)
Fact: There are 594 chapters before Psalms 118
Fact: There are 594 chapters after Psalms 118
Add these numbers up and you get 1188
What is the center verse in the Bible? (Psalms 118:8)

The Psalm ends on the reminder that the power and greatness of God's word does not rest only in its literary brilliance. Its greatness and glory is in the fact that God comes to us and seeks us in and through His word.

The first and fifth verses in a stanza often state the same theme followed by a statement of opposition, affliction or conflict, and the final (eighth) verse tends to be a transition introducing the next stanza.

"He never repeats himself; for if the same sentiment recurs it is placed in a fresh connection, and so exhibits another interesting shade of meaning. The more one studies it the fresher it becomes. It is loaded with holy sense, and is as weighty as it is bulky." C. H. Spurgeon. Spurgeon liked this Psalm so much, he said, "we might do well to commit it to memory."

Rev. H. Venn: "This is the Psalm (Psalm 119) I have often had recourse to, when I could find no spirit of prayer in my own heart, and at length the fire was kindled and I could pray," (from Charles Bridges on Psalm 119)

Prayer isn't passive, it's active. It's really doing something. Prayer isn't the least we can do, it's the most.

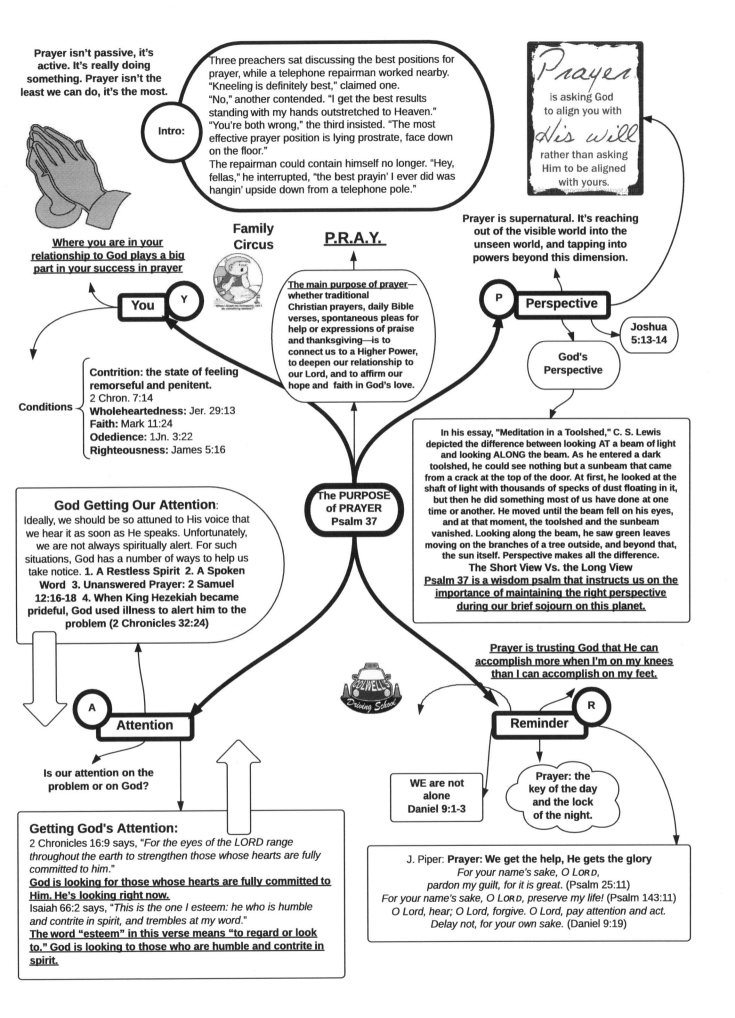

Intro: Three preachers sat discussing the best positions for prayer, while a telephone repairman worked nearby. "Kneeling is definitely best," claimed one.
"No," another contended. "I get the best results standing with my hands outstretched to Heaven."
"You're both wrong," the third insisted. "The most effective prayer position is lying prostrate, face down on the floor."
The repairman could contain himself no longer. "Hey, fellas," he interrupted, "the best prayin' I ever did was hangin' upside down from a telephone pole."

Prayer is asking God to align you with *His will* rather than asking Him to be aligned with yours.

Family Circus

P.R.A.Y.

The main purpose of prayer—whether traditional Christian prayers, daily Bible verses, spontaneous pleas for help or expressions of praise and thanksgiving—is to connect us to a Higher Power, to deepen our relationship to our Lord, and to affirm our hope and faith in God's love.

Prayer is supernatural. It's reaching out of the visible world into the unseen world, and tapping into powers beyond this dimension.

You Y

Where you are in your relationship to God plays a big part in your success in prayer

P **Perspective**

God's Perspective

Joshua 5:13-14

Conditions
Contrition: the state of feeling remorseful and penitent. 2 Chron. 7:14
Wholeheartedness: Jer. 29:13
Faith: Mark 11:24
Odedience: 1Jn. 3:22
Righteousness: James 5:16

The PURPOSE of PRAYER Psalm 37

In his essay, "Meditation in a Toolshed," C. S. Lewis depicted the difference between looking AT a beam of light and looking ALONG the beam. As he entered a dark toolshed, he could see nothing but a sunbeam that came from a crack at the top of the door. At first, he looked at the shaft of light with thousands of specks of dust floating in it, but then he did something most of us have done at one time or another. He moved until the beam fell on his eyes, and at that moment, the toolshed and the sunbeam vanished. Looking along the beam, he saw green leaves moving on the branches of a tree outside, and beyond that, the sun itself. Perspective makes all the difference.
The Short View Vs. the Long View
Psalm 37 is a wisdom psalm that instructs us on the importance of maintaining the right perspective during our brief sojourn on this planet.

God Getting Our Attention:
Ideally, we should be so attuned to His voice that we hear it as soon as He speaks. Unfortunately, we are not always spiritually alert. For such situations, God has a number of ways to help us take notice. 1. A Restless Spirit 2. A Spoken Word 3. Unanswered Prayer: 2 Samuel 12:16-18 4. When King Hezekiah became prideful, God used illness to alert him to the problem (2 Chronicles 32:24)

Prayer is trusting God that He can accomplish more when I'm on my knees than I can accomplish on my feet.

A **Attention**

R **Reminder**

Is our attention on the problem or on God?

WE are not alone Daniel 9:1-3

Prayer: the key of the day and the lock of the night.

Getting God's Attention:
2 Chronicles 16:9 says, "*For the eyes of the LORD range throughout the earth to strengthen those whose hearts are fully committed to him.*"
God is looking for those whose hearts are fully committed to Him. He's looking right now.
Isaiah 66:2 says, "*This is the one I esteem: he who is humble and contrite in spirit, and trembles at my word.*"
The word "esteem" in this verse means "to regard or look to." God is looking to those who are humble and contrite in spirit.

J. Piper: **Prayer: We get the help, He gets the glory**
For your name's sake, O LORD,
pardon my guilt, for it is great. (Psalm 25:11)
For your name's sake, O LORD, preserve my life! (Psalm 143:11)
O Lord, hear; O Lord, forgive. O Lord, pay attention and act.
Delay not, for your own sake. (Daniel 9:19)

Intro: Most of us are familiar with Ted Turner, the cable television millionaire. Turner, at the American Humanist Association banquet, where he received an award for his work on the environment and world peace, openly criticized fundamental Christianity. He said, "Jesus would be sick at his stomach over the way his ideas have been twisted." He went on to say, "I've been saved seven or eight times. But, I gave up on it, when, despite my prayers, my sister died. The more I strayed from my faith, the better I felt!"

Ted Turner is dead wrong, but he is perfectly reflecting the attitude many hold concerning God and the matter of prayer. Many people will pray about something for a while and when the answer doesn't come when they think it should, they just throw up their hands in defeat and say, "What's the use?" Many of us wouldn't admit that tonight, but we have done the same thing! This passage is a challenge to that notion!

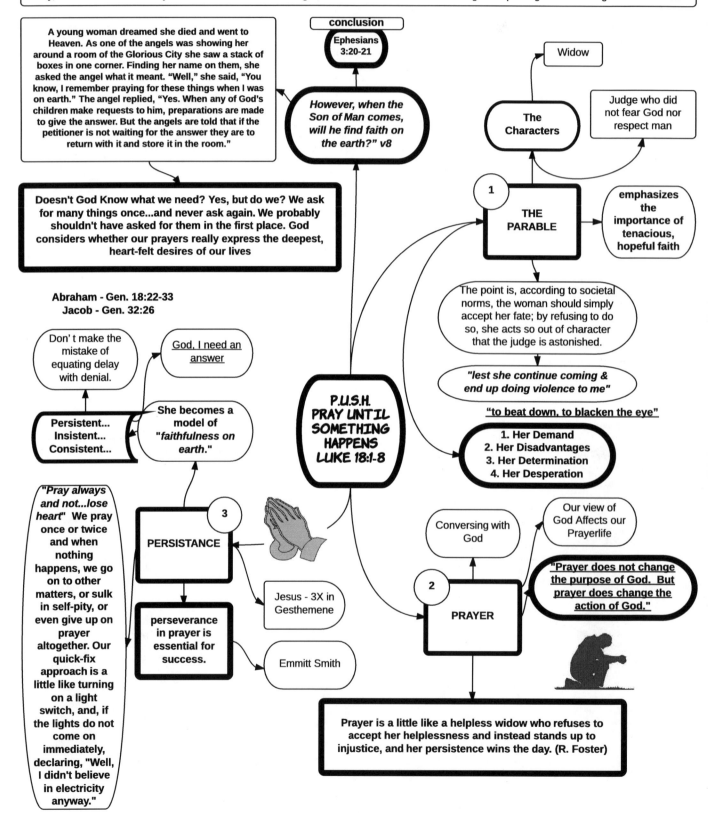

A young woman dreamed she died and went to Heaven. As one of the angels was showing her around a room of the Glorious City she saw a stack of boxes in one corner. Finding her name on them, she asked the angel what it meant. "Well," she said, "You know, I remember praying for these things when I was on earth." The angel replied, "Yes. When any of God's children make requests to him, preparations are made to give the answer. But the angels are told that if the petitioner is not waiting for the answer they are to return with it and store it in the room."

Doesn't God Know what we need? Yes, but do we? We ask for many things once...and never ask again. We probably shouldn't have asked for them in the first place. God considers whether our prayers really express the deepest, heart-felt desires of our lives

conclusion
Ephesians 3:20-21

However, when the Son of Man comes, will he find faith on the earth?" v8

Widow

The Characters

Judge who did not fear God nor respect man

1

THE PARABLE

emphasizes the importance of tenacious, hopeful faith

The point is, according to societal norms, the woman should simply accept her fate; by refusing to do so, she acts so out of character that the judge is astonished.

"lest she continue coming & end up doing violence to me"

"to beat down, to blacken the eye"

1. Her Demand
2. Her Disadvantages
3. Her Determination
4. Her Desperation

Abraham - Gen. 18:22-33
Jacob - Gen. 32:26

Don't make the mistake of equating delay with denial.

God, I need an answer

She becomes a model of "*faithfulness on earth.*"

Persistent... Insistent... Consistent...

P.U.S.H.
PRAY UNTIL SOMETHING HAPPENS
LUKE 18:1-8

"*Pray always and not...lose heart*" We pray once or twice and when nothing happens, we go on to other matters, or sulk in self-pity, or even give up on prayer altogether. Our quick-fix approach is a little like turning on a light switch, and, if the lights do not come on immediately, declaring, "Well, I didn't believe in electricity anyway."

3

PERSISTANCE

perseverance in prayer is essential for success.

Jesus - 3X in Gesthemene

Emmitt Smith

Conversing with God

Our view of God Affects our Prayerlife

2

PRAYER

"Prayer does not change the purpose of God. But prayer does change the action of God."

Prayer is a little like a helpless widow who refuses to accept her helplessness and instead stands up to injustice, and her persistence wins the day. (R. Foster)

CONCLUSION: One day you and I were going about our daily business and someone we had a relationship with let us down...One day you and I became proud of ourselves, a little too proud...One day you and i began to think we were worthless, that we couldn't make a difference...and we let these "wild gourds" poison our lives...There was *death in the pot*...**BUT before it was too late we realized that God, through Christ could provide the antedote...Will we let him?**

Background & Introduction:
- **Famine for 7 years**
- **What they ate they had to find in the woods**
- **Wild Gourd...indiginous to the area...size of an orange**
- **obviously resembled something that was edible**
- **when he picked the gourd and began to cut it up and put it in the soup, no one objected**

JIffy Mart sausage ...read ingredients: "cow lips"

We humans are very picky about what we allow in our stomachs. ..but not as careful about what we allow in our hearts...3 wild gourds we innocently allow in our lives, but if not caught in time can be poisonous and deadly...

Some people believe that low self-esteem is appropriate for Christians. They think that being humble means feeling worthless. None of us meets God's standard. We all fall short. WE are finite and fallible. We are sinful. None of us deserves God's favor. These are statements about our spiritual condition. We should not feel self-sufficient. We need God and his grace desperately. While we are correct to judge ourselves unworthy. GOD MAKES US WORTHY. We were created by God and our creation was called Good. God's grace given to us through the sacrifice of his Son, restores us to perfection in God's eyes. Many of us need to understand that biblical truth on an emotional level.

lack of trust: suspicion.

Low Self-esteem

The Wild Gourd 2 Kings 4:38-41

Mistrust

3 turtles

Opposite...not important... have nothing to contribute

often when we have been wrong...trusting becomes difficult

www.humanforsale.com You are worth exactly $2,224,998

Edward Kimball... Dwight L Moody... FB Meyer... J. Wilbur Chapman... Billy Sunday... Mordecai Ham... teenager named Billy Graham (Edward Kimball)

Takes a long time to build trust...but usually just one incident to lose

We are humans... we're going to make mistakes...

Pride

It may start out very innocently... grows... better to forgive

God doesn't cause trouble and adversity, but He uses trouble to refine some humility in us. While trouble causes some people to raise their faces to heaven and become bitter, others bow their knees before God and become better

Luke 14:1-11

It must be a very important truth because...3x in Bible: Prov. 3:34, James 4:6, 1 Peter 5:5 - "*GOD Opposes the Proud, but Gives Grace to the Humble.*"

Nothing wrong with taking pride in accomplishments. .... **BUT** when we allow it to boil and stew...it too can become poisonous...

Dr. George Borders

Latin word for humility is "humus" = "ground"...The humble person is the one who lives on the ground floor and Looks UP to God

"It is a strange fact of the human race that we all need somebody to look down on"

"It is better to have faith in everybody and be deceived occasionally than to mistrust everybody and be deceived almost constantly." — Christian D. Larson

CONCLUSION: If you were to look at Rembrandt's painting of The Three Crosses, your attention would be drawn first to the center cross on which Jesus died...the crowd...facial expressions...finally your eyes would drift to the edge of the painting and catch sight of another figure, almost hidden in the shadows. Art critics say this is a representation of Rembrandt himself, for he recognized that he was also there...We were there...not off to the side in the shadows, but on one of those crosses...and we have a choice about which cross is ours. **That choice depends on what you see...WHO you see...1,2 or 3...eyes of compassion.**

In 1991, Pizza Hut unknowingly offered some divine guidance through their Atlanta billboards. Joyce Simpson, and Atlanta fashion designer, claimed to receive an answer to her prayers in the middle of a fork full of Pizza Hut spaghetti. She prayed for a divine sign to help her decide on whether to stay in the church choir or quit and sing professionally. While driving past the billboard she claims to have seen Michelangelo's version of Jesus' face in the strands of spaghetti hanging from the fork. FORTUNATELY for Joyce, she saw Jesus. Other people claim to have seen Willie Nelson.

Nietzche once s "The last Christian upon a cross." He saying that when died so did Jes dream...his hope desire for the wo disagree...but doe world?

Everyday we have a choice in what we see. That's what we find in Luke's gospel. There were 3 crosses on Calvary's hill. We often see paintings of the three crosses. The one in the center is usually larger than the other two. I don't believe tat was the case. The crosses looked the same. And yet the frame of mind of the 3 who hung on the crosses that day were very different. There were 2 thieves and there was the Lord. We don't know the names, ages or background of the 2 thieves. We do know they were guilty and deserved punishment. Matthew tells us that they both joined in and mocked Jesus along with the crowd. But something happened to one of them. One began to see the man on the middle cross as the Lord. He pleaded for help, forgiveness and pity. IT ALL COMES DOWN TO WHAT THE THREE ON THE CROSSES SAW. THE CHOICE THEY HAD TO MAKE WAS WHO THEY SAW. **We have the same choice.**

To the Father...To the thief...

3

One Man Saw Others (v34)

He saw the lost crowd and he saw the thief...

1

Hanging right next to the one who could have saved him. The other thief recognized his foolishness...

One Thief Saw Only Himself (v39)

Tom Sine once wrote: convinced that often world doesn't take Christians seriously because we are so m like the world; caught the same miserable rat of self-seeking consumerism and materialism."

One man died IN sin. One man died TO sin. One man died FOR sin.

Who Do You See?
Luke 23:32-43

The thief on the cross saw only hmself...He didn't see the Messiah. He didn't see who he was or what he could do. His only interest was in himself

The first word Jesus spoke from the cross was a word of forgiveness...The second word was an answer to a prayer...and a promise

Can we honestly say tha do any different? Who d see? At times, we see ourselves.

That very day, this thief who was not fit to live on earth according to the Roman govt., went to be with the Lord. There is no greater picture of salvation through grace. This man had no goodness in him to merit salvation. He could join no church nor be baptized. He had no time nor opportunity to live out the teachings of Jesus. No Bible, no Christian parents, no church...and yet he believed...he trusted...he gained salvation. The men beside Jesus were both criminals/thieves...the difference lies in the fact that one thief believed in Jesus Christ and one didn't. One man saw Christ...the other didn't. One man was lost, the other was saved, Jesus died for them both.

2

One Saw the One Hanging on the Center Cross (v41)

Both Matthew & Mark tell us that in the beginning both thieves riduculed the Lord. But during the 6 hours they were on the cross, one thief saw that something unusual was taking place. He recognize that this one beside him was not dying for Himself but for others. Many scholars believe that these 2 men were partners of Barabbas. He knew Barabbas should be on that cross beside him...not this man. This man was dying for Barabbas...but he also seemed to realize tat he was dying for him. He recognized the transaction between this man and God...then he turned to him in faith.

This thief went:
1. From sin to the cross
2. From the cross to Christ 3. With Christ into eternity

When he saw Christ hanging beside him, he had: (1 awakened respect for God, (2) A realization that he sinner getting what he deserved and (3) A realizatio this man hanging beside him had the power to lead into eternity...Then he admitted his sin and threw hir on the mercy of God. Then he said "*Jesus, remen me when you come into your kingdom*"

The difference between what they saw and the consequences:
1. On thief saw the Lord...the other saw only himself
2. One thief tuned out the voice of God...the other listened
3. One thief saw his own sinfulness...the other didn't
4. One thief tuned out the cry of conscience...the other responded
5. One thief went with Jesus...the other was eternally separated from him

Heb 4:12 *For the word of God is quick (or alive), and powerful, and sharper than any two-edged sword, piercing even to the dividing asunder of soul and spirit, and of the joints and marrow, and is a discerner of the thoughts and intents of the heart.*

The writer of Hebrews wants us to know that the word of God is alive, living, active, effective, energetic, efficient, & powerful!

Kelly Stickel: 6 Benefits to Bible Reading

The final acceptance of the recognition of the 66 books of the Bible as Scripture took place at the Senate of Carthage in A. D. 397.The doctrine of canonicity is the church's affirmation of the belief that the 66 books of the Bible comprise the only inspired books that there are. And because they are inspired, no other books are; they have a unique divine authority by which we follow in our life and belief what they teach.
What criteria were used to determine the canon of Scripture?
1. Written by a recognized prophet or apostle (Hebrews)
2. Written by those associated with recognized prophet or apostle (Luke/Acts)
3. Truthfulness (Deut. 18:20-22)
4. Faithfulness to previously accepted canonical writings - This is where Hebrews shines, in terms of the Church's acceptance of it. Hebrews not only agrees with, but helps explain and bring to greater clarity, what has been taught in the Old Covenant
5. Confirmed by Christ, prophet, apostle (e.g. Luke 24:44; 2 Pet. 3:16)
6. Church Usage and Recognition

The Bible will keep you from sin or Sin will keep you from the Bible

Bruce Metzger: "The canon is not an authoritative collection of books, but a collection of authoritative books

Thy Word

That I may not Sin against Thee

There is POWER against Sin

Ex. - Jesus' temptation experience
1. Stones to bread
2. Pinnacle of the Temple
3. Mountain
(Deut 8:3, Deut 6:13, and Deut 6:16)

The Bible is one of the greatest blessings bestowed by God on the children of men. It has God for its author; salvation for its end, and truth without any mixture for its matter. It is all pure.
John Locke

The Bible is like a telescope.

Optical telescopes
Radio telescopes
X-ray telescopes
Gamma-ray telescopes
High-energy particle tele
Other types. Different types of telescope, operating in different wavelength bands, provide different information about the same object. Together they provide a more comprehensive understanding.

The Word in the Heart Psalm 119:10-16 (11)

60 miles an hour?! But that's impossible! I've only been driving for 15 minutes!

Bunell, FL

I know the Bible is inspired because it inspires me.
Dwight L. Moody

We should read and study the Bible because it is God's Word to us. The Bible is literally "God-breathed" (2 Timothy 3:16). In other words, it is God's very words to us. There are so many questions that philosophers have asked that God answers for us in Scripture. What is the purpose to life? Where did I come from? Is there life after death? How do I get to heaven? Why is the world full of evil? Why do I struggle to do good? In addition to these "big" questions, the Bible gives much practical advice in areas such as: What do I look for in a mate? How can I have a successful marriage? How can I be a good friend? How can I be a good parent? What is success and how do I achieve it? How can I change? What really matters in life? How can I live so that I do not look back with regret? How can I handle the unfair circumstances and bad events of life victoriously?

The Best Thing, in the Best Place, for the Best of Purposes

Proverbs 4:23 *Keep thy heart with all diligence; for out of it are the issues of life.*

I have hid in my Heart

George Barna wrote The State of the Church in 2002. Barna conducted a survey of self-pronounced Christians and here's what he found about their knowledge of the Bible. These are Christians.
• 48% could not name the four Gospels.
• 52% cannot identify more than two or three of Jesus' disciples.
• 60% of American Christians can't name even five of the 10 Commandments.
• 61% of American Christians think the Sermon on the Mount was preached by Billy Graham.
• 71% of American Christians think "God helps those who help themselves" is a Bible verse.
George Barna said, "Americans revere the Bible, but by and large they don't know what it says. And because they don't know it, they have become a nation of biblical illiterates."

1. watch what we see
2. watch what we hear
3. watch what is influencing us

As Mary treasured in her heart what she heard about and saw in her son...no one could ever take it away from her...

The act of hiding God's Word in one's heart is not just memorizing it, but by living in full devotion to the Lord.

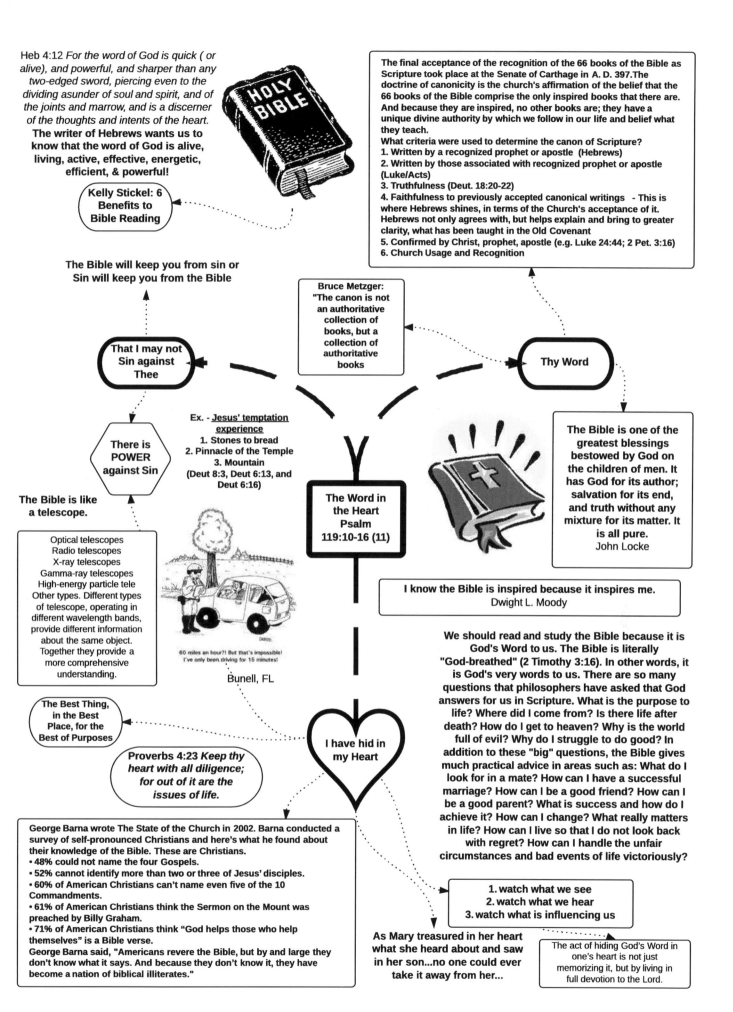

SEEING FAR ENOUGH AHEAD

Eight-year-old Frank had looked forward for weeks to this particular Saturday because his father had promised to take him fishing if the weather was suitable. There hadn't been any rain for weeks, and as Saturday approached, Frank was confident of the fishing trip. But, wouldn't you know it, when Saturday morning dawned, it was raining heavily and it appeared that it would continue all day. Frank wandered around the house, peering out the windows and grumbling more than a little. "Seems like the Lord would know that it would have been better to have the rain yesterday than today," he complained to his father who was sitting by the fireplace, enjoying a good book. His father tried to explain to Frank how badly the rain was needed, how it would make the flowers grow and bring much needed moisture to the farmers' crops. But Frank was adamant. "It just isn't right," he said over and over.

Then, about three o'clock, the rain stopped. There was still time for some fishing, and quickly the gear was loaded and they were off to the lake. Whether it was the rain or some other reason, the fish were biting hungrily and father and son returned with a full string of fine, big fish.

At supper, when some of the fish were ready, Frank's mom asked him to say grace. Frank did--and concluded his prayer by saying, **"And, Lord, if I sounded grumpy earlier today it was because I couldn't see far enough ahead."**

Introduction & Conclusion:

It is important to realize the Meaning of what we are doing:

We Look: Backward, Upward, Around, Inward and Forward

Is Jesus' death a good thing or a bad thing?

Sorrowful Aspects

Bigger picture: Best news possible

RETURN 1 COR. 11:26

REMEMBRANCE LUKE 22:19-20

...of Jesus

...of Jesus

Shows us how much God loves us

We look Forward

The Meaning of the Lord's Supper Mark 14:22-26

We Look Backward

(1) Jesus will come again for those who love him. (2) Jesus calls his followers to be ready all the time. (3) No one knows the day or the hour.

How do you receive a gift that involves personal sacrifice? With Great Gratitude! Love...Joy!!!

REALIZATION

...of a *Present Relationship* with Jesus

A Memorial...not a Funeral

and what that present relationship means:

How often do you examine yourself in light of Christ?

We look Inward

1 Cor. 11:28

The Lord's Supper helps us to look **Upward**, to Christ, and be mindful that true life can only be in him and with him.

The story is told of a college professor who visited the Fiji Islands. Being agnostic, he critically remarked to an elderly chief, "You're a great leader, but it's a pity you've been taken in by those foreign missionaries. They only want to get rich through you. **"No one believes the Bible anymore. People are tired of the threadbare story of Christ's dying on a cross for the sins of mankind.** They know better now. I'm sorry you've been so foolish as to accept their story." The old chief's eyes flashed as he answered. **"See that great rock over there**? On it we smashed the heads of our victims. **Notice the furnace next to it**? In that oven we formerly roasted the bodies of our enemies. **If it hadn't been for those good missionaries and the love of Jesus that changed us from cannibals into Christians, you'd never leave this place alive You'd better thank the Lord for the Gospel. Otherwise, we'd already be feasting on you. If it weren't for the Bible, you'd now be our supper"**

By his death and resurrection, He Conquered Death Hebrews 2:14-15

Ancient Israel looked back at the Passover...We look back at the cross...

Hold up receipt: This means the price has been paid!

BUT WE ALSO LOOK **Around**...WHEN WE ARE AWARE THAT JESUS LIVES IN US, WE ALSO PAUSE TO THINK WHAT KIND OF HOME WE ARE GIVING HIM.

Your mom's coming home...

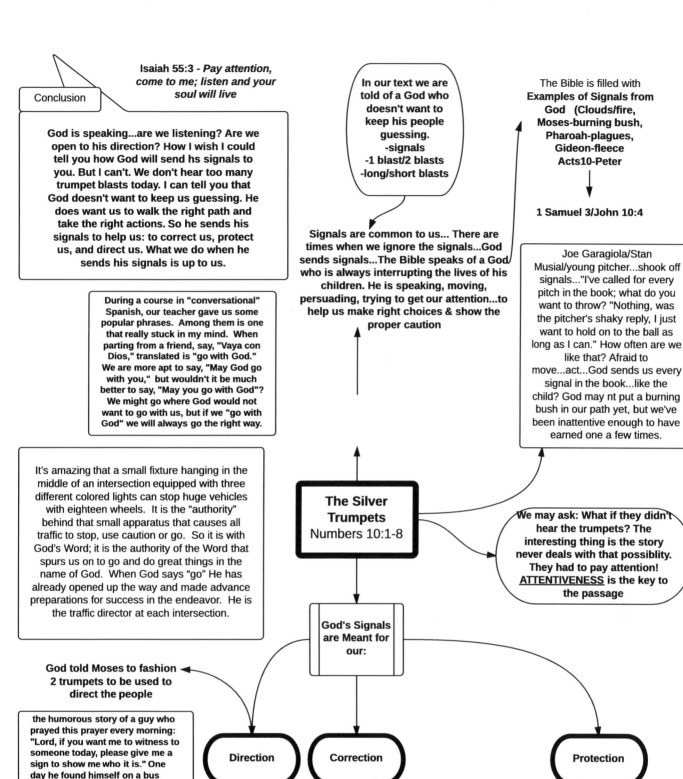

Isaiah 55:3 - *Pay attention, come to me; listen and your soul will live*

Conclusion

God is speaking...are we listening? Are we open to his direction? How I wish I could tell you how God will send hs signals to you. But I can't. We don't hear too many trumpet blasts today. I can tell you that God doesn't want to keep us guessing. He does want us to walk the right path and take the right actions. So he sends his signals to help us: to correct us, protect us, and direct us. What we do when he sends his signals is up to us.

In our text we are told of a God who doesn't want to keep his people guessing.
-signals
-1 blast/2 blasts
-long/short blasts

The Bible is filled with **Examples of Signals from God** (Clouds/fire, Moses-burning bush, Pharoah-plagues, Gideon-fleece Acts10-Peter

1 Samuel 3/John 10:4

Signals are common to us... There are times when we ignore the signals...God sends signals...The Bible speaks of a God who is always interrupting the lives of his children. He is speaking, moving, persuading, trying to get our attention...to help us make right choices & show the proper caution

During a course in "conversational" Spanish, our teacher gave us some popular phrases. Among them is one that really stuck in my mind. When parting from a friend, say, "Vaya con Dios," translated is "go with God."
We are more apt to say, "May God go with you," but wouldn't it be much better to say, "May you go with God"?
We might go where God would not want to go with us, but if we "go with God" we will always go the right way.

Joe Garagiola/Stan Musial/young pitcher...shook off signals..."I've called for every pitch in the book; what do you want to throw? "Nothing, was the pitcher's shaky reply, I just want to hold on to the ball as long as I can." How often are we like that? Afraid to move...act...God sends us every signal in the book...like the child? God may nt put a burning bush in our path yet, but we've been inattentive enough to have earned one a few times.

It's amazing that a small fixture hanging in the middle of an intersection equipped with three different colored lights can stop huge vehicles with eighteen wheels. It is the "authority" behind that small apparatus that causes all traffic to stop, use caution or go. So it is with God's Word; it is the authority of the Word that spurs us on to go and do great things in the name of God. When God says "go" He has already opened up the way and made advance preparations for success in the endeavor. He is the traffic director at each intersection.

The Silver Trumpets
Numbers 10:1-8

We may ask: What if they didn't hear the trumpets? The interesting thing is the story never deals with that possiblity. They had to pay attention! **ATTENTIVENESS** is the key to the passage

God's Signals are Meant for our:

God told Moses to fashion 2 trumpets to be used to direct the people

the humorous story of a guy who prayed this prayer every morning: "Lord, if you want me to witness to someone today, please give me a sign to show me who it is." One day he found himself on a bus when a big, burly man sat next to him. The bus was nearly empty but this guy sat next to our praying friend. The timid Christian anxiously waited for his stop so he could exit the bus. But before he could get very nervous about the man next to him, the big guy burst into tears and began to weep. He then cried out with a loud voice, "I need to be saved. I'm a lost sinner and I need the Lord. Won't somebody tell me how to be saved?" He turned to the Christian and pleaded, "Can you show me how to be saved?" The believer immediately bowed his head and prayed, "Lord, is this a sign?"

Direction

Correction

Protection

Paul on Road to Damascus Acts 9:1-8

Scottish Reformation/Spider The young man would later write: "To God, a spider's web is like a stone wall."

Conclusion

I have been preparing and preaching using mind maps for 20+ years. I enjoy preaching, but I enjoy preparing messages even more. I think this is because I never know where the topic or text will take me as I map it out. It's like unearthing a treasure (not that my sermons are worthy enough to be called treasures). I just find it enjoyable discovering where the Spirit will take me as I prepare the messages.

The messages are original, although I may have used basic outlines that are not completely original. In other words, if a sermon has 2 or 4 points, I may have heard those points through someone's sermon and then I took them on a different path than the original preacher used. I made them personal to me and my congregation.

Feel free to use any of the sermons included in this book. I hope you will try mind mapping your sermons and discover how enjoyable the preparation, as well as the preaching, can be.

Feel free to contact me as well: reece.sherman@gmail.com.

I have a website www.sermonmindmaps.com , I would love to include your sermon on the site. I will give you full credit. My plan for the site is to have a place where preachers can go and both share and get ideas for messages. So please email me your sermon mind maps.

I told you that I use Lucidcharts, but I have also used Mind Meister as well as Mind Manager in the past. There are many good mind mapping software applications that can be used. Find one you are comfortable with.

Made in the USA
Las Vegas, NV
27 July 2023

75310921R00017